From The Ashes:
Modern Application of
Traditional Martial Arts Concepts
And Techniques

From The Ashes:
Modern Application of
Traditional Martial Arts Concepts
And Techniques

Tom Gillis

Tom Gillis
2015

Copyright © 2015 by Tom Gillis

All rights reserved. This book or any portion thereof may not be reproduced or used in any manner whatsoever without the express written permission of the publisher except for the use of brief quotations in a book review or scholarly journal.

First Printing: 2015

ISBN 978-0-9939421-0-5

Tom Gillis
118 Cimarron Grove Road
Okotoks Alberta Canada T1S 2H1

www.ftsma.com

Ordering Information:

Special discounts are available on quantity purchases by corporations, associations, educators, and others. For details, contact the publisher at the above listed address.

U.S. trade bookstores and wholesalers: Please contact Tom Gillis Tel: (403) 829-7897; or email tom@ftsma.com.

Dedication

To all of my past and present martial arts and combatives teachers. From some of you I learned how to do things. From some of you I learned what not to do.

Table of Contents

Foreword 10

Preface..12

Training Model and Tactical Priorities..............................14

Fitness and Nutrition...28

Strikes 46

Balance Disruption...64

Completing the Puzzle...88

Percussion and Precision Weapons.................................106

Ground Fighting..120

Articles of Interest..142

Foreword

Having known Tom for many years has allowed me to see how a once mislead young man can turn his life around through proper instruction and dedicated teaching. Tom began his training in the warrior arts in order to acquire a deeper understanding of his own life as well as the psychology of those around him. He has magically and proficiently attained a life of self discovery that has transformed him into an amazing practitioner.

This book is fundamentally a testimony of his life as a student and, at the forefront of being a student, his willingness to learn. The focus is on three practical aspects of martial arts practice: techniques, tactics and the philosophies thereof.

Tom brilliantly captures the intimate connection within these fundamental principles by expanding on them both through modern practice ideals and the old ways of his most earnest schooling; his Budo. The brilliant triangular model of the five pillars of Budo is a reflection of the years of dedicated practice and willingness that he has encompassed as an eager investigator of the truth regarding The Arts.

After rather humble beginnings in the martial arts, he found his way to training with me by allowing himself to take on a holistic approach to understanding and willingness to in-depth study. Tom and I have been training together for many years now and have travelled together on various occasions to study under the traditional teachers of Japan.

On his quest, he has also travelled the Continent of North America to train with some of the leading experts in the fields of combat analysis and law enforcement. The instructors that Tom has trained are a living legacy of his ability to pass down the greatest of the martial truths.

The compilation of all of the related arts will make Tom a prominent figure in the future of warrior arts on this continent. His contributions to both human development and martial development, especially in its unification of the traditional Eastern way with the modern Western approach, will benefit humanity across the line.

I highly recommend that every individual, family and martial arts' community read this book as well as seek Tom out to spend time with him while he still teaches openly. May this book and all of its concepts provide its readers with abundant food for thought and sufficient fuel for practice on the way to a long and fruitful warriors quest.

Jay Creasey
Kanushi of Usagi Jinja

Preface

The contents of this book have been in the making for over 20 years. That's how long I've presently been involved in martial arts. While not all of that time were structured and formal, and certainly not all of it was taken seriously, my thoughts, particular fighting and teaching style, and opinions have been forged over that entire time.

For many years students, friends, and colleagues urged me to produce a written piece. Until now I never thought that anyone would be particularly interested in what I have to say. After all there are authors, teachers, and practitioners who have been training for longer than I've been alive.

Recently however events have led me to believe that sharing all of our voices is what will keep our arts alive. The old days of secrecy are dead. Martial artists no longer fight each other for nation or resources. Instead we share more common ground than we do contested or adversarial.

For the most part those who train do so for 3 reasons. The first is a love of the training and the arts. The second self preservation from a criminal and scavenger element of our society. And thirdly is for contest of fame and fortune in a ring. Out of those 3 groups only the last wouldn't want to openly share information, and this text probably isn't for them anyways.

So who is it for? It's for the warriors who want to keep their arts, their families and loved ones, and themselves alive. In this work I'll share with you what I believe are some basic martial arts lessons from a variety of schools and systems hundreds, if not thousands of years old, and how I've modernized them to fit today's world.

I hope you enjoy it and someday will share your voice and add to the conversation.

> **Training Model and Tactical Priorities**
>
> It is crucial that before learning physical techniques participants have a firm understanding of how to apply a traditional martial arts training model. This model is not what it seems to many people engaged in training today. As a matter of opinion most of the schools and students I see skip 80% of the model and jump to the last 20%
>
> Also included in this chapter are my Tactical Priorities. This is the first application of Tactics in this book and are easy to remember. After this chapter all the following material will focus on the Training Model and Tactical Priorities.

Training Model

Contrary to popular belief, martial arts and combative training do not focus solely on techniques. Traditionally warrior ethos and creeds, such as Bushido in Japan, were developed as part of the warriors' education. Traditional training in many systems around the world and throughout the ages included a system of ethical rules to follow, laws and expectations of the land, military tactics, and an ability to move and use your body. Often it was technical training that was used to develop a soldier's ability to fight and move. The graphic below illustrates that Ethics should be the foundation for martial arts training, not techniques. Techniques however are the tools used to teach the other foundational steps below them. They are a culmination of all the levels of training below them coming together in a moment. Techniques are like the tip of an iceberg. They're the part of martial arts that people can see and are the most obvious.

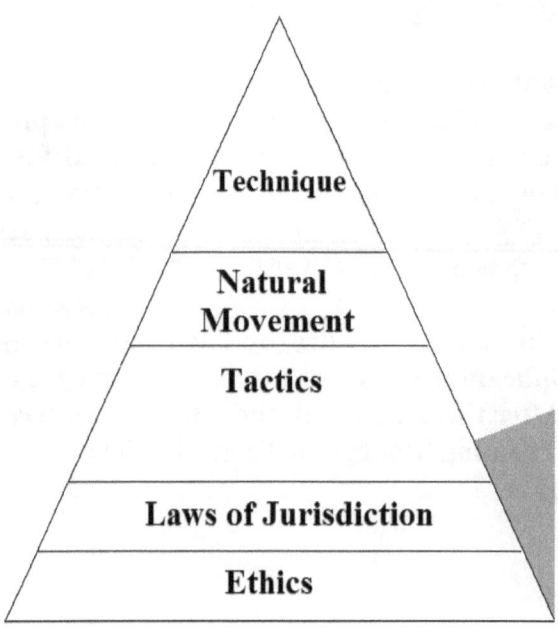

Ethics

The foundation for all training is **Ethical Behavior**. In ancient warrior cultures different codes of ethics and behaviors were developed to help soldiers deal with taking life and sacrificing their own in battle. These various codes of ethics were also developed to set cultures apart and ensure that soldiers did not develop psychopathy or other mental illnesses due to the stress of battle and warfare.

Ethical behavior means knowing AND doing what's right to protect life, **AT ALL TIMES**. This includes your life and the lives of EVERYONE else. This includes doing what you can to protect your adversary even in combative situations and definitely post conflict when you're safe. This means that at no time is it acceptable for you to take any actions that unnecessarily cause harm to any person.

This means taking unnecessary risks (i.e. speeding unnecessarily) are not acceptable, and the onus is on you to hone your skills to be able to protect life at all times. This is the highest calling for anyone who trains and is what separates Martial Artists from those who simply do martial arts.

Proper training that includes ethics as part of the training regime goes beyond just training schema for the typical **perceived stimulus: react** paradigm. It teaches students to develop a sense of focus and to be present in all situations and make conscious decisions based on the totality of circumstances. There are many documented cases of people who received training making reasonable mistakes in situations that have caused serious injury and in some circumstances unnecessary death. Instead the goal of training should be to instill a sense of **presence** in situations which encourages you to process the environment and make rapid **conscious** decisions. This level of proficiency takes time and effort but with hard work and dedication it is possible.

Law

Warriors have a duty to lead by example by following the laws, rules, regulations, and policies in effect. Remember however that the law cannot violate Ethical Behavior. In some jurisdictions, even in western nations, there are situations where you may be permitted to kill someone to protect property. According to our ethical code however property can never be more important than life, so even in these jurisdictions the expectation would be that you don't execute that particular right.

The onus is on the individual to research, know, and understand the law and follow it.

Tactics

Traditional martial training transmitted an understanding of tactics to students. Too often in modern martial arts we see trainers and students developing techniques in isolation from tactical principles. An example of this would be pulling someone down on top of you and wrapping your legs around them in a street fight. If the opponent suddenly arms themselves, has friends, or even if the environment isn't very sanitary, this can result in serious injury very quickly.

One thing that can help you to avoid Tactical Errors is to ask yourself what is the purpose of your training. For example a student engaged in Japanese Sword training for personal enjoyment and meditation will have a different set of tactics than a Filipino Martial Arts student who has a short period of time to learn how to survive a machete attack.

Some examples of tactics found throughout this book include (but aren't limited to);

- Shielding and cornering
- Angular Movement
- Changing elevation
- Jamming opponent's attacks before they have time to initiate
- Controlling space
- Engagement and disengagement
- 5 point balance manipulation
- Circumnavigation

Natural Movement

Any physical material taught in a class must follow rules of Natural Movement. This means it is imperative that you are constantly evaluating material and asking if what you're learning violates these rules.

The Rules for Natural Movement are;

- **Limbs are Springs**. The legs are responsible for lifting, and moving and work best when they have a slight flex in them. The knees should never be locked while moving. When punching the elbow should maintain a slight flex. Locking out the joints effects the body's ability to move well and can cause hyperextension injury.

- **Balance**. Maintain balance by keeping the head over the hips and back straight. Keeping your eyes up and alert to your surroundings will help to keep a straight back.

- **Respect your Center Line**. Limbs don't cross your own center line, and if they do correct it immediately. This means that while moving your feet should never be crossed. When moving left the left leg should move first by pushing off the ground with the right and vice versa.

- **Joint Stability**. The less a joint moves the more stable it is. One way to tell the natural position of a joint is to stand relaxed with your arms loosely at your sides and examine the way the joints align. While moving they should maintain this alignment. For example many people twist their wrist while punching so that the hand is horizontal to the ground. If you stand naturally and lift your arm you'll notice that your hand is vertical (thumb points up) for example.

- **Arms push and legs pull**. By understanding the most powerful and efficient use of the body you can maximize power and strength generation. To learn what this rule means try this exercise;

With a partner grab their wrist and step back away from them extending your arm. Try to pull them towards you with just your arm and have them resist slightly. Now repeat the exercise but this time start close to your partner and hold your elbow to your core. Now step back and pull them with your legs. Notice a difference?

Now stand back from your partner and extend your arms and put your hands on their chest. Have your partner resist as you push with your legs. To learn how to push properly stand closer to your partner and put your hands on their chest with your elbows close to your core. Keep your feet firmly planted on the ground and push with your arms by extending forwards with your elbows.

- **The Head is the Bodies Steering Wheel**. Where the head leads the body will follow. One of the most efficient ways to know where someone's body will go is to know where their eyes are looking. This means that to maintain an upright stable posture your own eyes should be up and aware of your surroundings. Not looking at the ground. This also means that if you can direct an opponent's vision in a particular direction you can manipulate their balance in that direction.

Technique

When Tactics are combined with Natural Movement in a manner that is Ethical, Legal Techniques are created. Techniques **CANNOT** violate any of the previous levels of development. Techniques that promote the students self discovery and promote a sense of balance, co-ordination, timing, precision, and power are best. A training regime in which techniques build on each other are more desirable than a training program where each technique is different.

When training techniques the goal is to practice them to the point where they exist in the brain stem, and not the pre frontal lobe. Sports science research indicates that an effective way to do this is to limit the amount of time that you work on a piece of material to approximately 20 minutes, take a break from that material, and then come back to it within an hour. This level of skill takes years to develop and tens of thousands of reps so you better be prepared to work for it.

Training Methodology Conclusion

Traditional martial arts training covered far more than just technical skill. Teachers and masters often recorded texts on tactics and ethos and not on technical skill. One such example is the Book of 5 Rings by Miyomoto Musashi and the Art of War by Sun Tzu. Neither of these texts provide any details to physical techniques but yet both are heavily laden with Tactics and Ethos. There is some mention in the Book of 5 Rings as to principles of Natural Body Movement.

The reason for this is simple. Both Sun Tzu and Musashi understood that the physical techniques are not the top priority and cannot be learned absent of other factors. Yet in todays martial arts training regimes there seems to be little discussion around these other non-technical factors.

In order to develop yourself as a warrior a comprehension of Ethics, Law, Tactics, and Natural Body Movement, *MUST* be in place. Developing techniques absent of these other factors is reckless and dangerous.

Tactical Priorities

There are 6 tactical priorities that will help you stay safe if you're ever attacked. In most instances it's the application of these priorities in conjunction within legal guidelines that dictate which tactics or techniques to use. Most people that are attacked and injured are attacked because they gave the subject the opportunity to hurt them. By following the Tactical Priorities you can reduce the chance that an assailant will hurt you.

The Tactical Priorities are;

Priority #1, Don't get hit.

Sport martial arts and combative martial arts differ greatly. In combative martial arts your first priority during any contact with an assailant should be to not get struck by that person. During street altercations there are no rules, no safety equipment, and often no one to help if you get hurt. Assailant's can deploy weapons and even in the case of an empty hand altercation you can't be sure of their intent or if and when they'll stop attacking. For this reason *the first priority is to not get hit*. The first hit in a street altercation might be the last. There are several tactics that you can use to maximize your chances of not getting hit;

- **Cover, concealment, and shielding.** Understanding the differences between cover, concealment, and shielding and using them effectively can greatly increase your safety. *Cover* is something that will hide you AND stop the threat from penetrating. It is accepted that something that will stop a bullet is cover. *Concealment* will allow you to hide yourself from the assailant but will not stop weapons from penetrating through. A car door in a gun fight is concealment. In situations where cover isn't available use items for shielding, such as chairs, tables, and wall corners. *Shields* provide an obstacle that a subject must navigate to reach you but won't necessarily stop weapons and don't block line of sight. By using shielding you can effectively slow down an attacker.

- **Move on 45, stay alive.** The use of angular movement can move you out of the way of incoming attacks and cause the attacker to recalculate where you are and how to continue an attack. Using 45 degree angular movement relative to a subject can also open opportunities for counter attacks and control techniques.

- **Threat cues.** Often assailant's who attack people display some threat cues just before the attack. An observant person will pick up on these threat cues and be prepared to take action. Threat cues include what is said, how it said, eye movement, clenched fists, and other cues of nervousness and anxiety. Don't fall into the trap of focusing on someone's eyes when talking to them. Watch the hands and the rest of their body/surroundings for threat cues. People who effectively read threat cues have been shown to have faster reaction time and in some cases are able to move with an assailant's attack instead of after it.

➢ **Maintain Distance.** Reaction time is defined as the amount of time between when something is observed, processed, a plan formulated, and motor neurons begin to initiate a motor response. You can increase the amount of time you have to complete this process by increasing the distance to a threat. The further the distance from an assailant the more time you'll have to react to their actions. This relationship can work against you too. If there is too much space from the subject they will have more time to react when physical control is attempted. The minimum distance maintained to a subject should be no less than a step and an arm's reach, greater depending on the situation.

➢ **Watch for Multiples.** Often time's people find themselves faced with multiple opponent's or opponent's with multiple weapons. This can be dangerous especially when the defender deals with the initial threat and then lowers their guard. For this reason it is important to remember that once a threat is recognized and neutralized to continue to look for others.

➢ **Keep your hands up.** Always during a confrontation you should remember to keep your hands up. An easy way to remember this is to use hand movement in front of your face or chest while talking. If a situation starts out as a verbal altercation and the assailant's actions become escalated the hands are in a position to fight from. If an assaultive altercation happens the hands should stay up at face level.

- **De-escalate when available**. The use of calm verbal communication can effectively de-escalate a situation and decrease your chance of injury. Staying calm and attempting to verbally deescalate a situation before they become physical can be very difficult. Verbal communication skills are just like physical skills, they require training and experience to be effective.

- **Disengagement.** Disengagement is a consideration that you may employ in an attempt to control a situation. If you cannot safely control a situation, or if disengagement would assist in controlling a situation with a lower level of force, you should disengage from the incident. Disengagement may not be possible in some circumstances. Environmental factors such as obstacles or barriers may physically prevent you leaving. As well, the distance between you and the assailant, and the weapon being used by the assailant may also eliminate the use of this option. Lastly, the safety of your family or others around you may dictate that disengagement is not an option.

Tactical Priority #2, Hit Back.

Hit Back means that you employ techniques to take the initiative and put an assailant on the reaction side of the situation. Often times however you won't know you're under attack until after it starts. Once you've determined that an attack is imminent and what actions are reasonable you can initiate techniques towards the assailant.

Tactical Priority #3, Finish the Fight.

Finish the Fight is situational and will change given the totality of the circumstances. The circumstances will dictate what action is *Ethical* and *Legal*. You must make a commitment before an altercation to never give up. *Every confrontation is winnable*. If something isn't working change tactics and continue on. Developing a winning mentality also includes preparing before you head out, maintaining a high degree of physical fitness, and using imagery and visualization

It should be noted here that in some instances priorities 1-3 happen simultaneously. For example if an attacker were to produce a knife and lunge at you and you move out of the way, deploy your own knife and cut the assailant, and the cut stops the assailant.

However the situation unfolds once the assailant is unable or unwilling to continue to engage in their assaultive behavior you must continue on to the second part of the priority list. It should be noted that depending on the situation priorities 4-6 might change order. They are provided below in a general format that will fit most situations:
Tactical Priority #4, Escape and Evade.

Once the other party/ies are unable or unwilling to continue to fight get to a safe location!

Tactical Priority #5, Call for help.

Depending on the lethality of the situation you might swap priority 4 and 5. If for instance if you or someone else are injured getting Emergency Services on the way might be more important. In the case of injuries the amount of time from when the injury occurred to when treatment begins can make the difference between life and death. For this reason it's recommended that as soon as possible you should call for help. In the best case scenario this would be before an altercation even began. Most attacks are ambushes however and calling for help before the altercation is often impossible.

Tactical Priority #6, Self aid/first aid.

As soon as safe to do so check yourself for injuries and then other people. Although you might want to help other people first it is impossible for you to treat someone effectively and ongoing if you're too wounded to help them.

For this reason give yourself a primary survey to assess the extent of your injuries first and then decide if you need to treat yourself or others first. This also means that you should maintain a high level of first aid knowledge.

Tactical Priorities Conclusion

During a violent situation following the 6 Tactical Priorities can help you make good decisions and maximize your safety. The 6 Tactical Priorities are Don't Get Hit, Hit

Back, Finish the Fight, Escape and Evade, 1st Aid/Self Aid, Call for Help. Depending on the totality of circumstances the priorities might change order. This framework is the first application of tactics and once these *Tactics* are combined with *Natural Body Movement* we will begin to develop *Techniques*. It is therefore crucial to keep these tactics in mind during your training and not to do or develop anything that violates them.

> **Fitness and Nutrition**
>
> **Hopefully one of your goals of training in the warrior arts is to enjoy a healthier more fulfilling life. Combatives is all about survival and living longer after all. Living a healthy lifestyle should be a part of that process.**
>
> **Being able to generate power, speed, strength, and endurance are all critical components of a fight also. You can possess all the technical skill in the world, but if you're gasping for breath in the middle of a fight it won't do you any good.**

Nutrition

Nutrition is a vital component to healthy living and combative performance. So much so that healthy eating was included in ancient martial arts training and conditioning. Masaaki Hatsumi's first attempt at creating a text for Ninjutsu was called Togakure Ryu. In it one of the first subject's covered was eating properly and how to exercise.

The importance of proper nutrition isn't a concept found solely in Ninjutsu or even Japanese Martial Arts for that matter. All traditional martial arts have their nutrition and fitness "secrets" passed down for generations that would give their students the upper hand in a fight.

Proper nutrition should have 3 goals:

Eliminate Toxins

What good is training to win a fight if you die from toxicity at a young age? The build up of toxins are related to several diseases including, but not limited to, Alzheimer's, obesity, respiratory illnesses, heart conditions, and various types of cancers.

Good nutrition therefore should seek to eliminate toxins by eating healthy food and drinking plenty of water.

Controlling Body Composition

Obesity is related to High Blood Pressure, Heart Disease, High Cholesterol, Heart Attack, Stroke, Back Pain, Arthritis, Infertility, and Gallstones just to name a few of the serious health conditions that are affected by poor body composition.

From the perspective of surviving a combative engagement with an adversary an obese body uses more energy in order to move and is able to generate less force than a healthy body.

Controlling body composition therefore must be a priority for anyone training in martial arts or other combatives.

Performance Variables

As mentioned above all the technical skill in the world can't get you safely through a fight if you're too exhausted to perform, or if your body can't generate power to deliver techniques. By focusing on performance, instead of just health or body image, we can become better combatants. There is a difference between being in shape, and being able to perform. I've witnessed this phenomenon several times as a martial arts teacher. New students will join a martial arts class who are in incredible shape but within 20 minutes of training they're exhausted. Meanwhile the student who's been training in martial arts for years, but doesn't look like they're in excellent shape, can perform for upwards of 8 hours at a seminar.

Nutrition and physical fitness training MUST HAVE a performance element and not just focus on health and body image.

Eating Properly

My goal in developing a nutrition plan was to give students something that was simple, that they could understand conceptually, and that they would stick with long term (hopefully for the rest of their lives). I myself have struggled with nutrition my entire life and had tried everything from counting calories, to cleansing, to restricting certain foods. Consistently I found that the more complex the process the better it worked for me short term, but it became too hard to maintain in my normal hectically busy everyday life.

It was with this in mind that I developed the following 10 Principles for Healthy Eating.

1. Stay close to nature

When I was in my late 20's I found myself going from a very active job to a very slow one where I spent most of my time sitting. I didn't realise that I should change my nutrition to suit the new activity level and I gained a lot of weight (nearly 60 pounds in 1 year). As a result I ended up with very high cholesterol levels and poor body composition. After an annual trip to my family doctor I decided it was time to make a change.

The first change I made was to eliminate fats and sugars (more on that next) and to eliminate processed foods. I continued with this process for nearly 3 years until the point where I was eating Organic foods. What I discovered was that I didn't experience as many emotional ups and downs, I slept better, had more energy, was able to perform at a higher level, and was better able to manage my weight and body composition.

When applying Principle #1, Stay Close to Nature, there is a simple process to follow;

- *Certified Organic Foods* are best. Certified Organic means that the producers must adhere to strict guidelines and the food, water, and soil that it grows in are tested regularly and must meet strict toxic levels. If the toxicity of the samples is above government regulations then that food producer loses their certification. This food has the lowest levels of toxins and the highest nutritional value. It costs more at a grocery store but because of the increased nutritional value you'll eat less.

- *All Natural Foods* are good. These foods are grown on farms or in gardens with limited application of pesticides, herbicides, or preservatives but don't meet the threshold to be certified organic. This is usually what you find at farmers markets. These foods are good for you but may still have toxins in them from the growing process.
- *Fresh Foods* are OK. Fresh Foods are whole foods that haven't been processed but are produced using modern means such as herbicides, pesticides, medications, steroids, artificial selection, and some preservatives. These foods can be deceptively toxic.
- *Processed Foods* are unhealthy. Processed foods include white flour or ground sugars, canned goods, and some pre-prepared items. These are generally low in nutritional value and high in toxins.
- *Artificial Foods* should be avoided. These include pre-prepared meals, artificial flavours and colours, most fast foods, and artificial sweeteners. These foods have very little to no nutritional value and are loaded with toxins and unhealthy fats.

When changing your nutrition identify where you are on this list and take time moving through the list towards Certified Organic Foods. For example when I started this process I was in between Processed and Fresh Foods. It took me 3 years to move to Certified Organic. Your brain is addicted to whatever it is you're used to consuming now. Your body has learned to become dependent on whatever chemical composition is in the food you currently live on. For this reason when you make a change there is a period of withdrawal from what you're used to and acceptance to what you're moving towards. This can make this process uncomfortable and difficult. Be prepared to be patient and take your time and you will feel and see results.

2. Avoid Sugars and Fats

A standard 1st World Nation diet is loaded with sugars, artificial colours and flavours, and fats to make food taste better. The result is toxic food that leads to obesity and multiple other health concerns and diseases. As it relates to performance, sugar is a fast burning energy source which means if it's your only fuel source when a fight starts you'll have a super burst of energy, but it will be short in duration and usually followed by a severe crash afterwards.

For these reasons sugars and fats should be avoided. Principle #2 CANNOT violate principle #1. This means that artificial oils and sweeteners cannot be used as a substitute. Once suggestions for sweetening food is to use organic honey in place of sugar, or coconut oil in place of butter. Methods such as these allow you to replace fats and sugars in your diet with healthy options without substituting taste and enjoyment. Most of my students actually report that they enjoy the healthy options more and are just as flavourful and even more flavourful than processed sugars and fats.

3. Variety is the Spice of Life

Too much of any type of food can be unhealthy. In my experiences with students who were vegetarians I noticed that many of them had a tendency to substitute soy products for everything. They ceased to be vegetarians and became soy-etarians. Too much soy has been attributed to an increase in estrogen. A dramatic increase in any body hormone leads in unbalance and is unhealthy.

In warmer climates a variety in produce is much easier than it is in colder ones. The body requires a variety of vitamins, minerals, anti-oxidants, proteins, healthy oils and fats, pro-biotics, and many other nutrients to achieve maximum health. These are obtained by ingesting a variety of colourful fruits and vegetables along with a variety of meats and other sources of protein.

4. No Fluids before Eating

The average human has approximately 500ml of Hydrochloric Acid (HCL) in their stomach. This stomach acid is responsible for efficient digestion of your food. If food isn't digested efficiently it can sit in the stomach and become rancid.

For this reason it's undesirable to dilute the stomach acid. Diluted acid isn't as efficient at digesting food. Generally fluids shouldn't be consumed for approximately 30 minutes before a meal.

5. Only 2oz of Meat in a Sitting

As mentioned above the stomach only holds 500ml of HCL. Meats are especially difficult to digest and it can take the HCL a lot of time to break them down. Particularly red meats. For this reason portions should be kept small so the meat doesn't sit in the stomach and become rancid. A simple guideline is to keep portions small enough to fit in the palm of your hand.

It's also important not to consume meats late at night before bed. As your body and brain slow down and prepare for sleep digestion also slows down. If your stomach is filled with meat as it slows down the contents might not be digested properly. This means that they'll sit in your stomach turning rancid and make you sick.

6. Chew Your Food

Particularly in North America there's a lot of pressure to multi task and rush through certain tasks. In my experience many of my students and clients rush through eating which results in them not chewing their food enough.

Chewing is the process of ingestion and is the first step in digestion. Large pieces of food take longer to digest and can result in food sitting in the stomach and becoming rancid. As mentioned above stomach rancidity can make you sick. Smaller pieces are easier to digest.

7. No Fluids with Your Meal

One of the best ways to make sure you're following Principle #6 is through Principle #7. When people drink fluids with their meals there can be a temptation to not chew food as much and "wash it down" with the fluids. If you don't drink any fluids with your meal it can force you to chew your food more.

8. Take Time to Relax Before Eating

In Principle #6, Chew your Food, we discussed the tendency to rush while eating. Also our brains don't differentiate between the stress of modern life and survival stress. One of the bodies' responses to stress is to decrease the digestion process to move resources to skeletal muscle.

Therefore if you're eating while stressed there isn't as much blood in the digestion system to digest food. This can lead to food sitting in the stomach and becoming rancid.

One of the best ways to reverse the effects of stress is with breathing techniques. Do 1 or 2 counts of relaxation breathing before your meal following this pattern; In for 4 seconds, hold for 4 seconds, out for 4 seconds, and hold for 4 seconds.

9. Time Sugars with Exercise

In Principle #2 we discussed avoiding sugars. This doesn't mean that every source of sugar can, or should, be eliminated from your diet. Sugars are an essential fuel source and building block for our body.

During exercise our body uses stored energy for the activity. Sugars consumed after exercise will aid in rebuilding tissue and replenishing energy stores in muscle. This is not an excuse however to consume copious amounts of refined sugars and unhealthy foods.

10. Drink Water

The human body is nearly 80% water. Water is essential to metabolize fat, grow muscle, and lubricate joints and smooth muscle (responsible for digestion). Even a small amount of dehydration can lead to a major drop in performance.

It is imperative to maintain hydration. I recommend to my students a minimum of 2.5 liters of water per day and to increase that by at least 1 glass (8 fluid ounces) while exercising and another glass for every cup of coffee consumed. Remember to not drink water at least 30 minutes before eating!

By following these 10 principles you will begin to see and feel a huge change in your body. I once had a student come to me for advice who was in her 60's and on 16 prescription medications. She followed the 10 principles for 6 weeks and her doctor took her off 13 of the prescriptions. Obviously this was an extreme case but it demonstrates the importance of proper nutrition and how powerful a simple conceptual understanding and application of those concepts can be. As you get healthier and feel better be sure to follow the advice of qualified medical doctors and don't stop taking any prescriptions until your doctor tells you it's ok to.

When to Eat

Not only is it important to appreciate and understand what and how to eat but also when. Throughout the day your body goes through a cycle. This cycle has been developed over hundreds of thousands of years. It's only been in the last 100 years that we can cheat the sun and stay up and active after dark. Before that when the sun went down if we weren't in shelter staying safe, warm, and dry, we were something else's dinner.

Understanding this cycle is important to maximize your potential gains from changes in diet. The following chart illustrates how to time your meals.

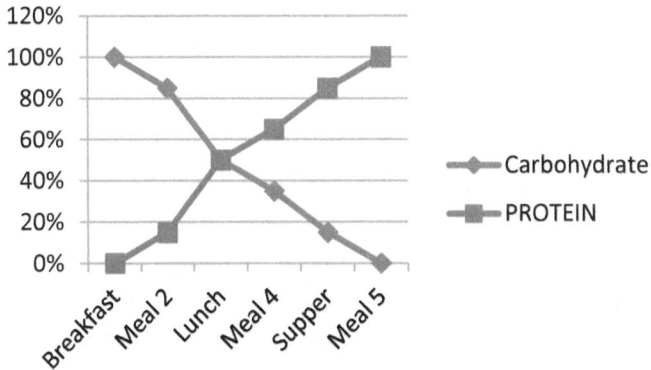

As you can see your day should start high in grains and fruits (carbohydrates) and throughout the day be replaced by meat and vegetables (proteins). Remember to time sugars with exercise when possible, drink plenty of water throughout the day, and not to eat meat before bed.

Nutrition Conclusions

Good nutrition is essential to the warriors' lifestyle. The goal of learning combatives is longevity and enjoyment of life. Being fit and healthy is an important part of that. Proper nutrition helps combat many lifestyle diseases that are found in western civilization as well as increase your ability to perform during a fight.

This chapter isn't meant to replace advice from a physician or qualified nutrition expert and doesn't even begin to cover the effects of supplements, micro nutrients, and targeted eating for performance. It's meant as a starting point only.

What is Fitness?

For today's warrior fitness should mean more than "being in shape." Looking good and being healthy isn't always the same thing. For this reason we must first define Fitness and look at all the components of fitness.

Component #1. Strength

Strength is the ability to generate force through muscular contraction. Examples of strength in combatives might include grip strength, ability to resist someone attempting to extend a limb, the ability to hold onto someone in a clinch situation, being able to lift a heavy object or person, or possibly being able to hold someone down in a ground fight.

Strength can greatly assist technical ability and can cause some serious problems for the other party to solve. Although it's not necessarily the most important factor in a fight it's a bonus if you have it.

Remember that a system is only as strong as its weakest link. This means that the major muscle groups of the arms, legs, body and neck will only generate as much strength as the minor auxiliary muscle groups and tendons and ligaments will support.

Component #2. Speed

Being able to move quickly in a fight is a bonus. Hand and foot speed can give you a huge advantage over your opponent. For the purposes of a fight *Speed* is the ability to accelerate a weapon or change positions quickly.

Component #3. Power

Depending on your fighting style *Power* is likely more important than *Strength*. *Power* can be defined in a fight as the ability to generate muscular contraction in a short period of time. *Power* is best thought as *explosivity*, your ability to hit hard and transfer energy. *Power* therefore has two components, *Strength* and *Speed*.

Like strength, power is partially dependant on technique and auxiliary support systems such as auxiliary muscle and tendon strength.

Component #4. Balance

Being able to maintain *Balance* in a fight is an important priority. If you're knocked down to the ground you just went from bad to worse. By maintaining skeletal relationship between your head, pelvis and legs, *Balance* is maintained. Some people develop good balance naturally, for everyone else it needs to be trained.

Component #5. Recovery Time

Being able to recover your breath, lower your heart rate, and decrease blood pressure after a fight are all very important. After a fight you may have to run, fight again, or assist someone else who needs aid. Being able to recover in a short period of time can greatly increase your chances of winning an altercation.

Component #6. Body Composition

Previously in the Nutrition section the importance of body composition was discussed and how important it is to long term health and enjoyment of life. Heart disease, cholesterol, diabetes, and obesity are serious health concerns in many industrialized nations.

Part of your fitness training should focus on burning fat and increasing muscle to increase body composition.

Component #7. Cardio Vascular Health and Endurance

Endurance is your ability to sustain activity for extended periods of time. One of the goals of training is to end an altercation quickly. In Chinese martial arts there's a saying, "a fight should not last more than 3 heart beats."

However in cases where a situation lasts for a prolonged period of time you must be physically prepared to go the distance.

Endurance training is also a great tool for maintaining Body Composition AND Cardio Vascular health. Keeping the heart, lungs, and blood vessels healthy and strong are important for living a long and happy life.

Component #8. Flexibility

I measure a martial artists' *flexibility* by their ability to dynamically move through a healthy range of motion without injuring themselves and without warming up first.

This is important to understand because in an altercation the other person isn't going to give you a chance to warm up. You might even be responding to a situation or an attack that began while you were asleep.

The goal of maintaining and increasing *flexibility* is to be able to move "cold." Also, as we age, one of the first components of fitness to deteriorate is our flexibility. This leads to decreased activity and a more sedentary lifestyle and also increases the likelihood of serious injury in our senior years.

Component #9. Physiotherapy

Undoubtedly when you train in martial arts and combatives your body is going to get beat up and injured. Physiotherapy movements should therefore be included in your routines. Examples might include leg extensions with toes pointed in or out to strengthen the sides of the knee, or running backwards and sideways to strengthen support groups in the legs.

Building a Training Program

A variety of training methods should be introduced to make sure that all 9 of the fitness goals are met. Type, Frequency, and Duration must all be taken into consideration when building a fitness training regime.

There are many different types of workouts that martial artists and combat athletes use to develop their fitness. It is foolish for someone training to hone their warrior skills to stick to one type of fitness training. This can lead to plateaus and only develops 1 aspect of your ability and potential.

The goal is to exercise 4 times per week, generally two days in a row with a rest day in between. Over the course of the week the entire body should be exercised using a combination of pushing and pulling movements to develop as many of the Components of Fitness previously discussed.

I use a variety of different methods during the week to try to cover many possible areas. Most of the time the resistance movements are done with *plyometrics* in mind (short and powerful), but sometimes they're done with *isometrics* in mind (slow and hold a contraction). About 50% of the time the resistance is from body weight or isometric tension and the other 50% of the time resistance objects. I favor kettle bells and other unbalanced weight objects to better simulate what I might feel during a fight.

Stretching should be done every day ***AFTER*** any physical activity for a cool down. Stretching ***IS NOT*** a warm up activity. Stretching can be completed by yourself and each position held for 30 seconds. It can also be done with a partner where the partner provides the hold and you push or pull into them building isometric tension.

Fitness Conclusion

This chapter is not meant as a guide to fitness. Rather it's an introduction of components for new students and a reminder for experienced students.

One of the biggest mistakes traditional martial artists make is not including fitness training in their regime. Combat sport athletes on the other hand spend at least 30% of their time developing their fitness.

Fitness has many different aspects for warriors and warrior training. All of these aspects must be understood and developed along with physical skills in order to be effective in a combat engagement. Developing skill without developing fitness is not enough to survive a violent encounter.

To really develop your physical fitness you should conduct your own research and contact a physical fitness specialist.

Strikes

There has been, and continues to be much controversy surrounding the idea of striking an adversary. It is thought that public perception looks unfavorably upon strikes because it appears like they're delivered out of anger, frustration, and panic.

This is not the intended motivation behind striking another person however. Rather strikes are used for two primary reasons. First they distract the adversary from staying strong in their structure and joints opening a window for follow up skeletal control, and second they give you an entry into establishing position and posture from which you can deploy follow up control methods.

Understanding Strikes

Strikes are an unreliable method of controlling someone. This is for a variety of reasons. First strikes primarily rely on a pain response. Because people have a wide spectrum of responses to pain it's unknown how anyone will respond. Secondly striking applies kinetic energy and then cycles off the target thereby not actually controlling anything or limiting someone's ability to continue to move.

In case studies from around the world subject's continue to assault their victims even after receiving multiple strikes. A goal orientated attacker can ignore the pain caused by being struck and continue their violent and illegal action.

For these reasons I do not think that strikes will cause any type of impairment in an adversaries ability to move their body or use their skeletal muscle. The majority of people who cease their assaultive action due to striking do it because they either choose to because of the pain of the strikes or because they're rendered unconscious.

Understanding how to strike is beneficial for two reasons however. First it can provide an opportunity for you to regain your structure and position in a fight. Most attacks are a surprise attack. This often puts the would be victim behind in terms of reaction time and most often results in them moving rearwards. A strike by its very nature moves forwards. For this reason strikes are an effective means of moving forwards again and reestablishing skeletal posture and maintaining balance as well as possibly offsetting the physical and mental balance of the attacker.

Secondly striking can create entry points to make the necessary attachments for follow up methods of skeletal control. Striking often allows a window of opportunity for follow up control methods because the subject, at least for a brief time, is distracted by the strike. In a best case scenario after receiving a strike a subject will decide to cease their violent action and stop fighting.

Technique 1. Straight Punch

- The straight punch is the primary strike that I use. It is applied with the striking foot forwards and with a vertical fist. The primary target is an opponent's face.

- To begin step forwards and raise the hands to the chest.

- Once the feet have stopped moving thrust the hand forwards maintaining a vertical fist while simultaneously dropping the center of gravity and slightly rotating the upper body from hips to shoulders and keeping the other hand elevated to protect the upper body and face. Your hand should follow a straight line from your chest to the target. Your arm should stay within the silhouette of your body.

- Make contact with a straight wrist and the flat of the fingers and knuckles.

- Push through the target and once the end of the strike is reached cycle the hand back in a straight line to the body.

- Remember to squeeze the forearm muscles enough to keep the wrist straight and maintain a slight flex in the elbow joint.

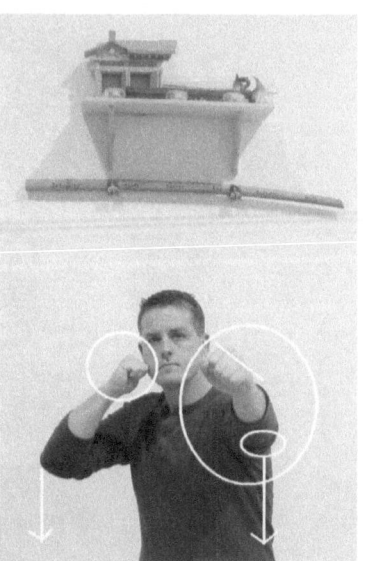

Technique #2. Palm Heel Strike

- The primary targets for the Palm Heel Strike are the opponent's upper chest or face. It is an excellent tool for knocking people back and gaining space. It is applied with the striking foot forwards.

- The delivery of the strike starts the same as the Straight Punch. To begin step forwards and raise the hands to the chest.

- Once the feet have stopped moving thrust the hand forwards. Open the fingers and pull them up and back so that they're pointing at the ceiling. Simultaneously drop the center of gravity and slightly rotating the upper body from hips to shoulders and keeping the other hand elevated to protect the upper body and face. Your hand should follow a straight line from your chest to the target. Your arm should stay within the silhouette of your body.
- Make contact with the base of the hand (the heel of the palm).

- Push through the target and once the end of the strike is reached cycle the hand back in a straight line to the body.

- I find this is one of the favored strikes by beginners because they don't have to worry about keeping the wrist strong. Because the fingers are pulled back the striking surface is right at the end of the radius and ulna bones.

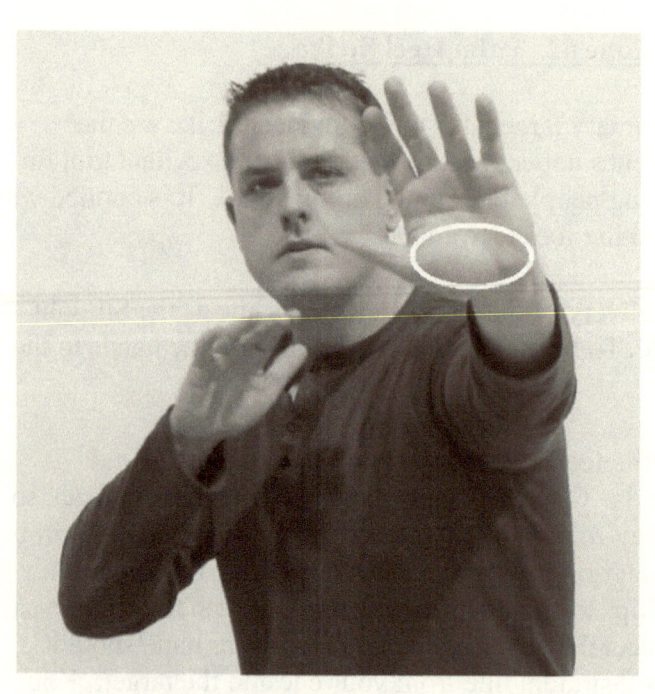

Technique #3. Hammer Fist

- The primary targets for the Hammer Fist are the subject's face or side of their head. It is primarily a close quarters strike and is primarily used when manipulating a subject's skeleton with the other hand.

- To begin the strike step forwards and raise the arms to the chest in a crossed fashion with the forward arm matching the forward leg and elbows bent.

- To deliver the strike rotate into the target and extend the elbow while dropping the center of gravity and closing the fist tightly while turning it so it's horizontal to the ground.

- Contact is made with the meaty portion of the hand under the pinky finger.

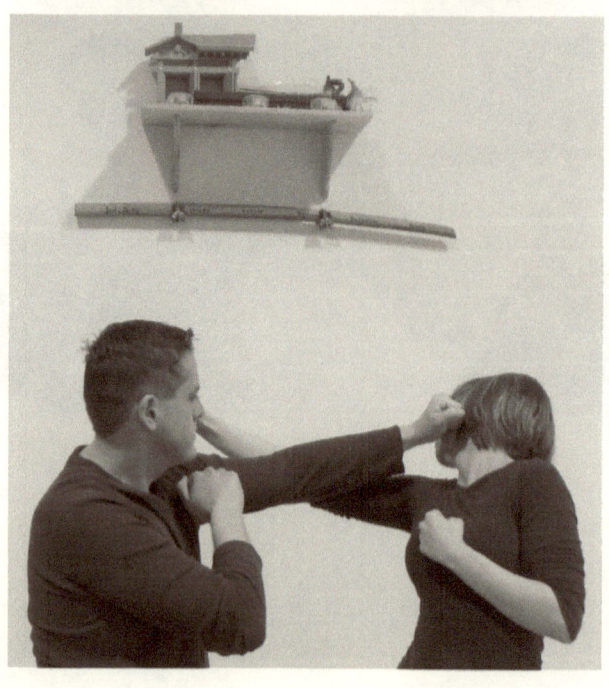

Technique #4. Elbow Strikes

- There are many different ways to utilize elbow Strikes. I primarily use 4 different methods all delivered at close quarters. They are the Outside Horizontal Elbow, the Inside Horizontal Elbow, the Uppercut Vertical Elbow, and the Rear Horizontal Elbow. Targeting is to the subject's head. Keep in mind however that because an elbow is such a hard striking surface and delivered at very close range, they can be added to a variety of close quarters fighting methods such as the ground fighting techniques which will be explored in chapter 7.

- All 4 delivery methods utilize some common concepts. They are body rotation, dropping center of gravity at time of impact, forward foot – forward weapon, and impact with the tip of the elbow.

- To deliver an Outside Horizontal Elbow step forwards and raise the corresponding arm, bent in at the elbow so the hand is touching the chest. Rotate the upper body from the hips through the shoulders while simultaneously dropping the center of gravity. Impact is made with the tip of the elbow and a follow through while balance is maintained.

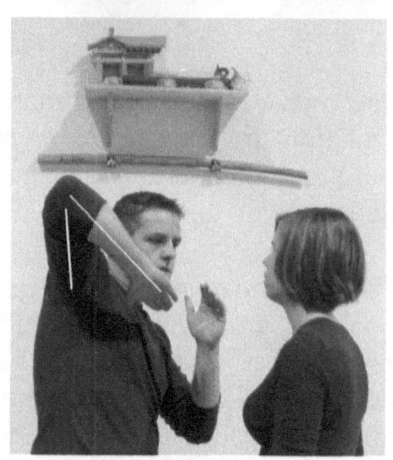
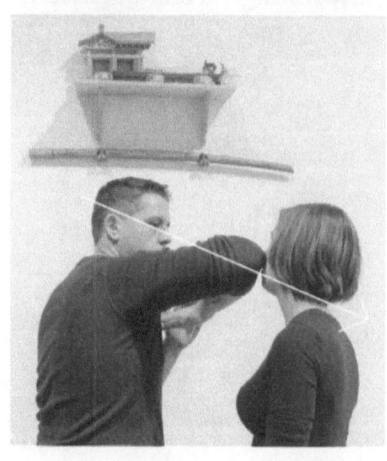

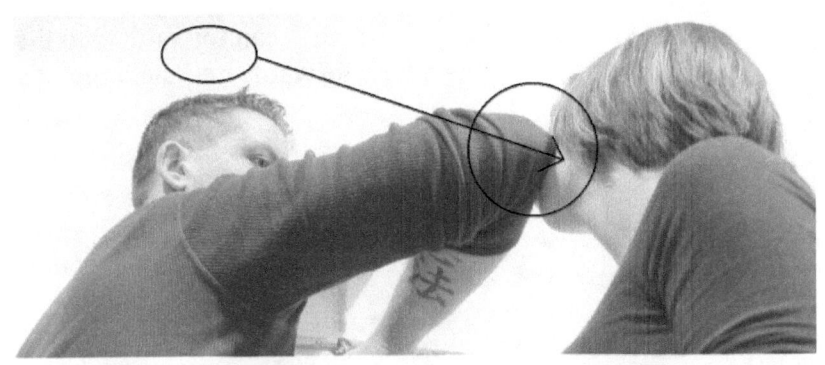

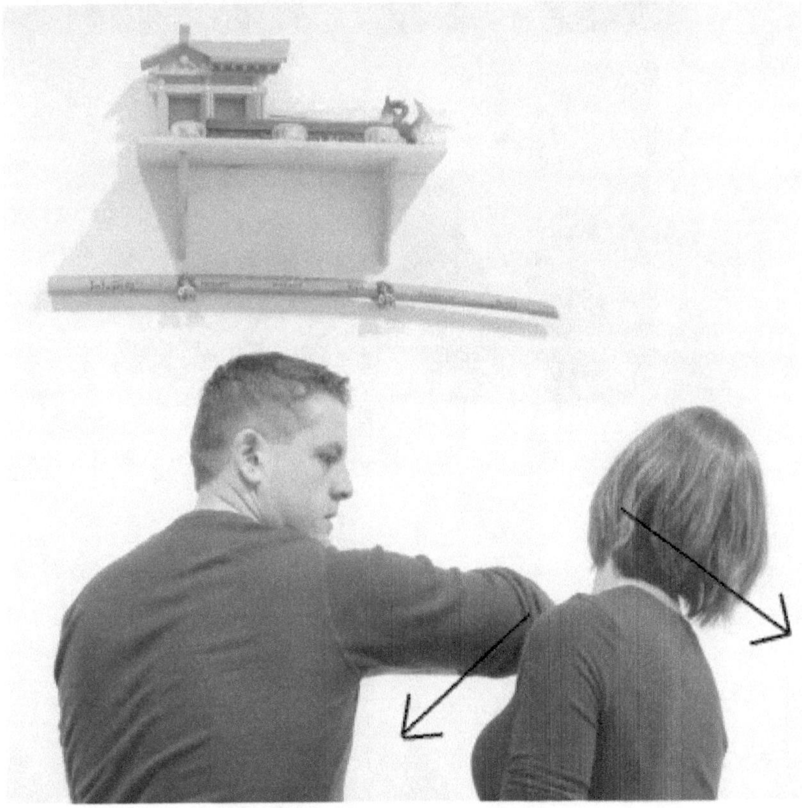

- To deliver an Inside Horizontal Elbow, begin where the Outside Horizontal Elbow finished. Lean forwards into the target while thrusting the elbow forwards into the target.

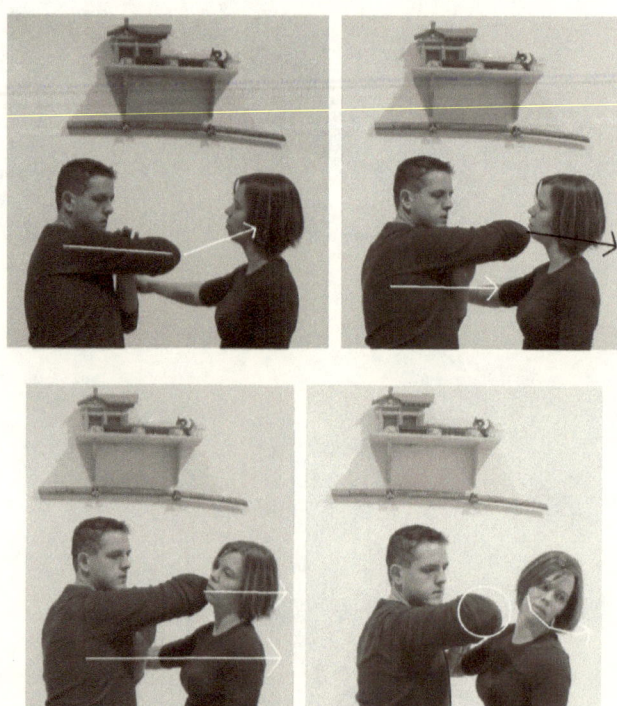

- To deliver a Uppercut Vertical Elbow begin once again by stepping forwards but this time tuck a vertical arm against the rib cage with a bend at the elbow so that the hand is touching the chest. Begin to lift the elbow through the shoulder while simultaneously lifting up onto the ball of the foot and rotating the hips. The primary target is under the subject's chin. Follow through by pointing the elbow straight to the sky.

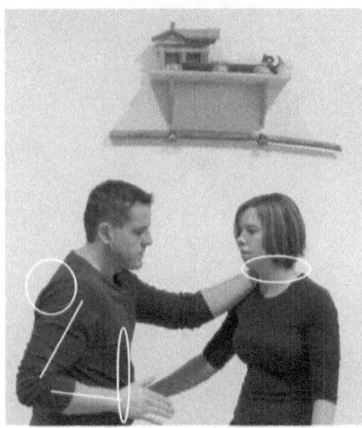
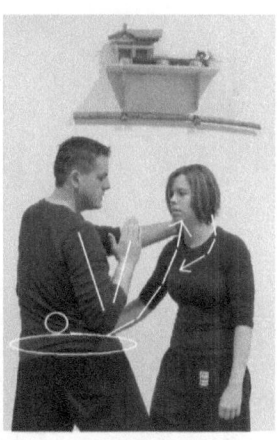
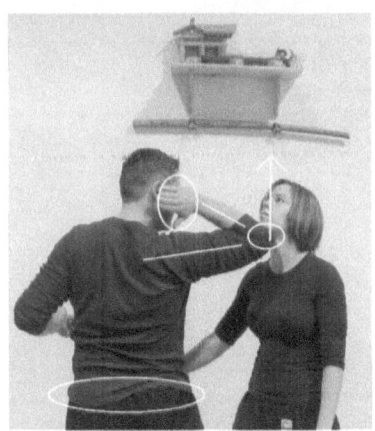

- To deliver a Rear Horizontal Elbow start by lifting the hands to the chest with elbows bent. Step rearwards with the foot that corresponds with the elbow you wish to strike with. Lift the elbow so that it's horizontal and rotate through the hips and shoulders while dropping the center of gravity. Impact is made with the tip of the elbow.

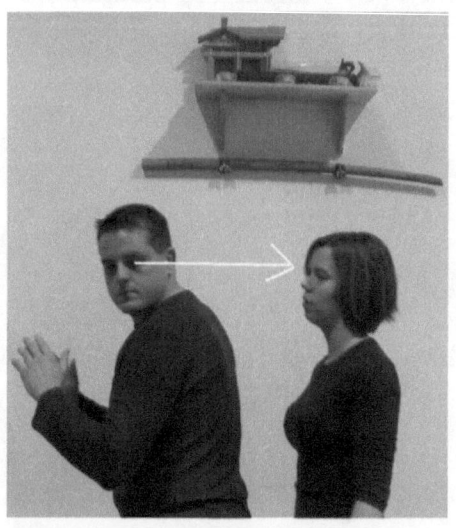

Technique #5. Knee Strikes

- Knee strikes are primarily used to strike a subject's legs to temporarily alter their base and structure. After a knee strike immediate skeletal manipulation and follow up control should be used.

- To deploy a Knee Strike first ensure a grip with the hands somewhere on the subject's arms or bodies.

- Next chamber the leg intended to apply the strike by stretching it rearwards.

- Deliver the strike by pulling the subject into it using the hands and thrust the tip of the knee through the intended target.

- The most effective target zones are the upper legs.

- Immediately after delivering the strike follow up with a control technique or takedown.

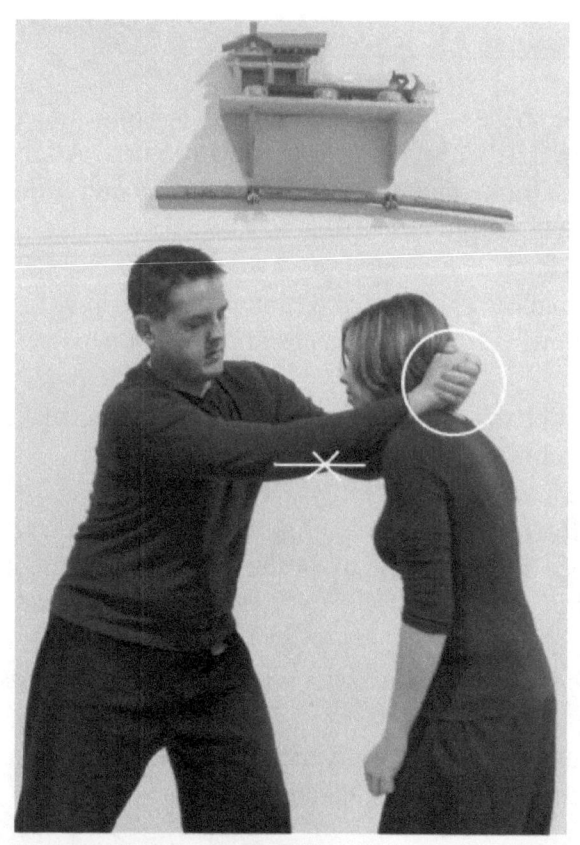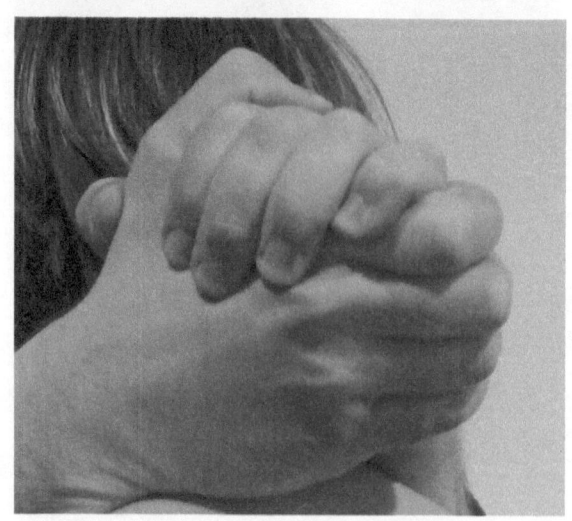

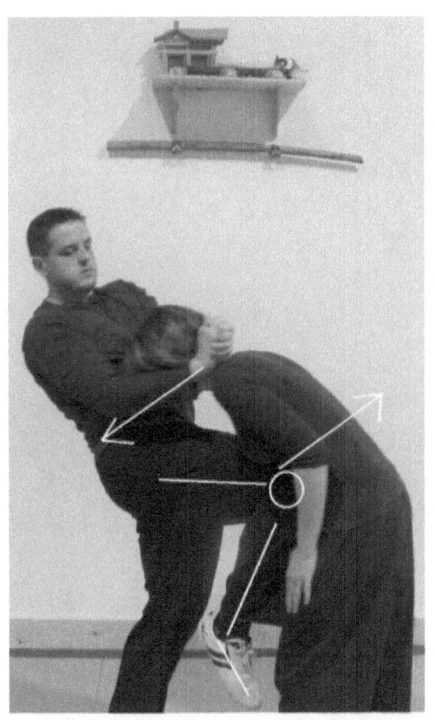

Conclusion

While applying strikes to someone can be beneficial to alter their mental or physical balance, strikes shouldn't be relied on to end a confrontation due to the spectrum of pain tolerance and the unreliability and unpredictability of the effectiveness of the strike. Strikes should never be delivered out of frustration or retribution but rather should only be applied as part of an overall strategy to manipulate the assailant's skeleton and open a window of opportunity for follow up control.

> **Balance Disruption**
>
> In many altercations your goal is to acquire a dominant position over the assailant. The most effective of these positional relationships is with the assailant lying on the ground on their front (Prone Position) and you standing on your feet.
>
> This for this reason it is critical you have an understanding of how to effectively control and disrupt an assailant's balance.

What is Balance?

Before practicing how to engage a subject with a takedown technique, it's important to have a conceptual understanding of what is meant by "balance". Too often I see students who are in such a rush to take their opponent down they compromise their own balance. Or while striking they'll be too concerned with generating power from the striking limb and will practically throw themselves into a strike. The only thing that keeps them from falling over is the opposite force from hitting their target. If they miss they may fall right over or at least stumble.

Balance is the natural relationship between the head, shoulders, hips, knees, and ankles. When these 5 points are lined up vertically you are in balance. Martial arts by its very nature are about movement. When one of these points moves the others must move in order to maintain the relationship.

Follow along with me for an exercise to help illustrate. Stand with your back against a wall, your heels, backs of your knees, hips, shoulders, and back of your head all touching the wall. Now without letting your hips, knees, or heels come off the wall begin rolling your back forwards by first touching your chin to your chest and then continue down the spine until your shoulders are well out in front of your body leaning over at the waist. How far did you get before you fell over and had to move part of your lower body?

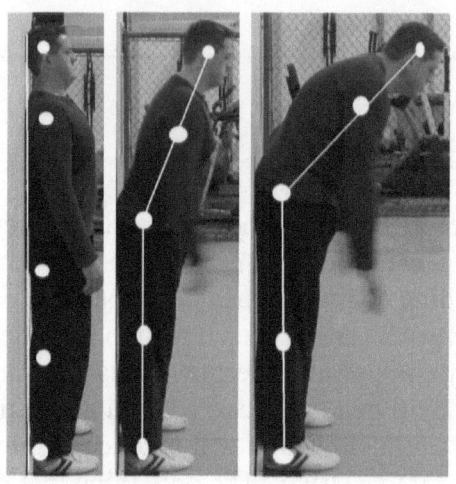

Now repeat the exercise but come away from the wall. As your shoulders lean forward allow your hips to extend rearwards. You should be able to get your head completely inverted and touch your toes without falling over. This movement exercise illustrates that when one part of the 5 balance points moves another one must also move to compensate to maintain the relationship.

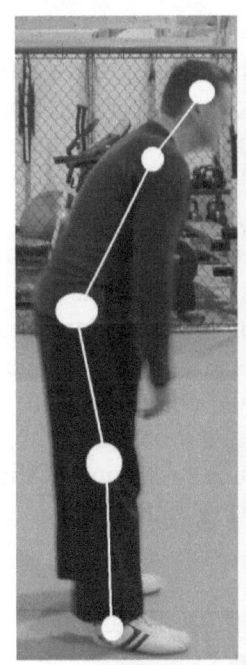
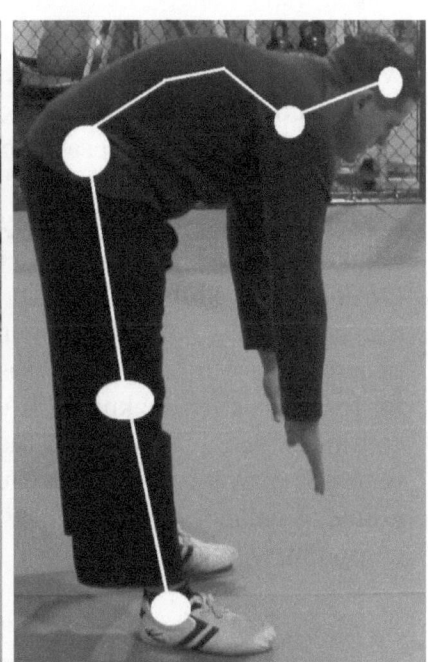
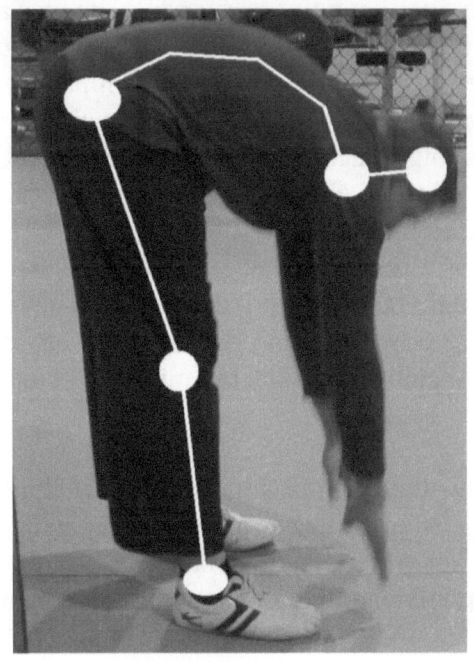

These rules of balance have to be taken into account when moving through techniques. If you move a part of your body too much and the compensatory points are unable to keep up you'll sacrifice your own balance. Let's examine a straight punch. New students load the punch and when they strike they throw their shoulder behind the strike. This leads to a chain reaction down the spine to the hips which also lean forward. Now they're bent over at the waist which extends the head to be too far forwards over the hips and the hips to be too far forwards over the knees. If the chain reaction continues the knees will lock out and be too far forwards over the ankles. Because every one of the 5 points of balance are tilted forwards balance is compromised.

Going back to our exercise, if my shoulders are moving forwards I need to compensate somewhere else by moving that point rearwards. The hips are the equivalent to the shoulders in the lower body. Therefore as I strike forwards my hips should adjust rearwards. However, if I shoot my hips straight back with straight legs as I punch my head will tilt forwards and I won't be able to generate any forwards force. Therefore my knees must compensate to my hips by bending slightly. If I punch in this manner not only do I maintain balance but I also generate more force because now I'm using gravity to my advantage AND more skeleton and skeletal muscle is being used to deliver the strike.

This therefore becomes the *"form"* for the straight punch. Maintaining form in your techniques is what will train you to maintain balance. Not following the forms will lead to disrupting your own balance which violates Rule #4 in our training model, *Natural Body Movement*.

Balance Disruption Techniques are those which disrupt the natural homeostatic state between the head, shoulders, hips, knees, and ankles in the opponent. This can be accomplished two ways; use of the limbs as levers, and disrupting spinal alignment by attacking 2 or more of the 5 points of balance.

With both methods it is critical to understand the most likely outcome of the technique to predict when and where a subject is going fall. Both methods can be accomplished with striking or pushing energy. When attacking the 5 points of balance it is important that scissoring energy is used. That means that if I apply force to 1 of the 5 points then an opposing force needs to be applied at another one. Without the opposing force the body will correct the posture and maintain balance.

Technique #1. Horizontal Rear Jaw Control

- Jaw control is otherwise referred to as Head Manipulation or Jaw Manipulation.
- Jaw control can be accomplished in several ways. Imagine that the subject sees the world calculated on two planes, a horizontal and a vertical. By manipulating the mandible (jaw) you are able to manipulate where the eyes look in relation to those 2 planes.
- A rear horizontal jaw control is performed from behind the opponent.

- The technique starts by extending your hands past the targets head and clasping them together one over the other.
- Begin to pull your hands back catching the target across the bridge of the nose and across the eyes.

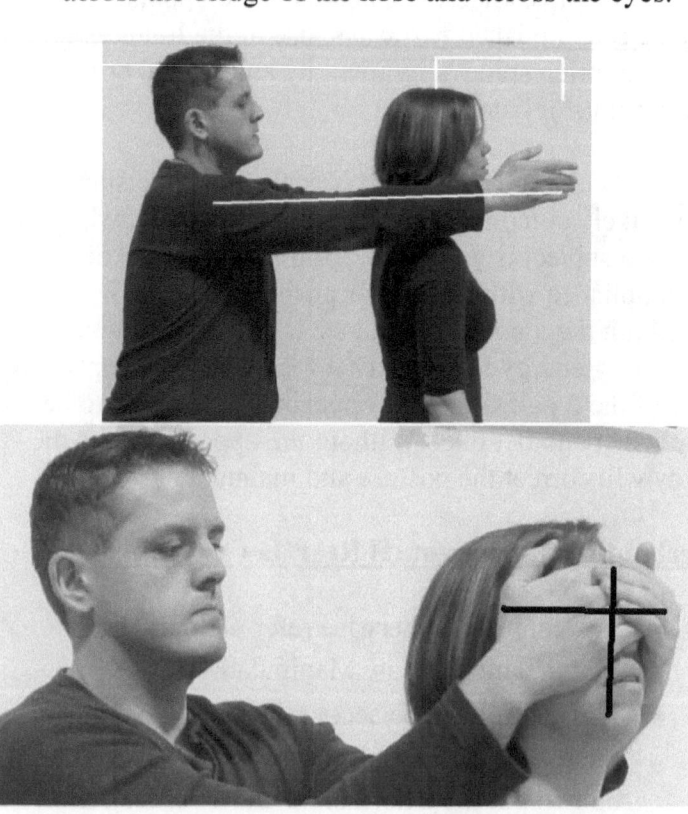

- Strike down into the subject's' shoulder blades with your elbows.

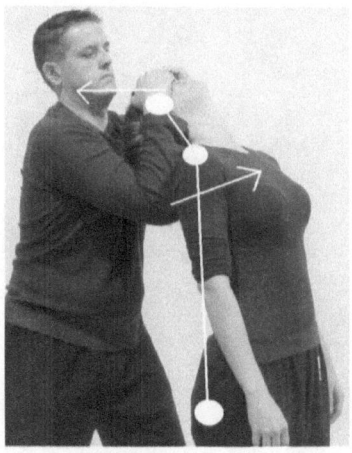

- Finish the technique by flaring their elbows up and to the side while pushing down forcing the other person to land on their back. Remember "head to heels" and push straight down not back into you.

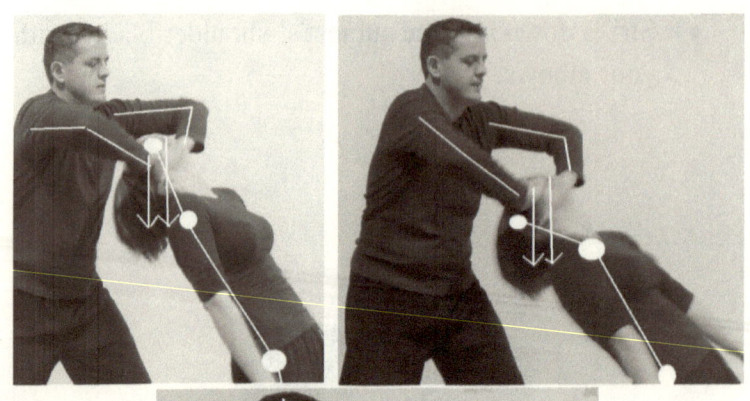

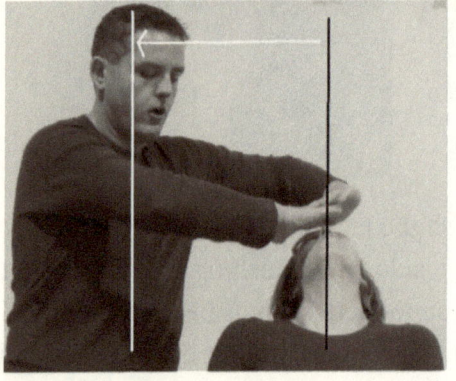

- Take into account space requirements and decide whether or not to stay still, step sideways or straight back while the opponent is falling.

<u>Technique #2. Horizontal Front Jaw Control</u>

- A front horizontal jaw control is performed from the inside position. It is often used to overcome rear jaw control resistance, or when fighting from the inside position.
- The technique starts by clinching your hands behind the subject's head and clasping them together one over the other.

- Pull your hands forewords and down to direct the opponent's eyes to the ground.
- Finish the technique by flaring your elbows up and to the side while pushing down forcing the subject to land on their stomach. Remember "nose to toes" and push straight down not forwards into you.
- Take into account space requirements and decide whether or not to stay still, step sideways, straight down or straight back while the subject is falling.

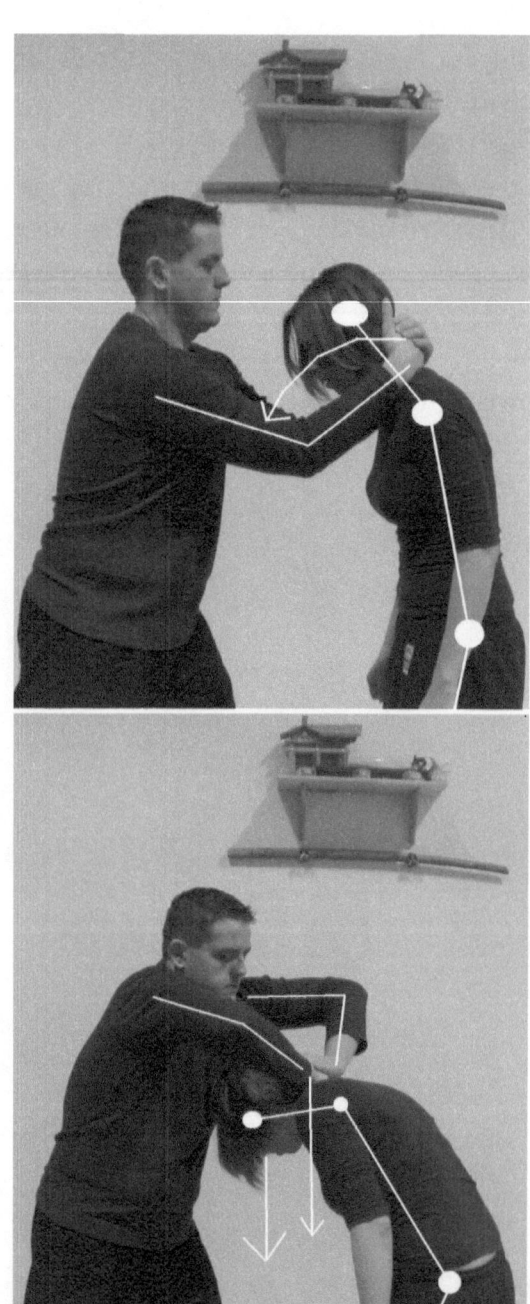

Technique #3. Shoulder and Knee Manipulation

- If the opponent is too tall for a Rear Horizontal Jaw Manipulation then the Rear Shoulder Pull with Knee Push technique can be used.
- A Rear Shoulder Pull with Knee Push is performed from the ambush position behind the other person.
- The technique starts by grabbing the target's shoulders at the trapezoids while simultaneously placing one foot on the back of the subject's mirror side leg with toes pointing out.

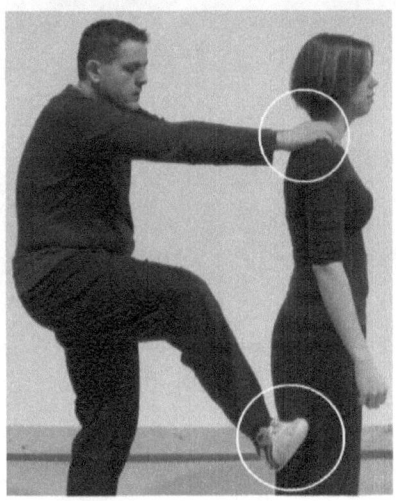

- Pull your hands back pulling their shoulders back while simultaneously pushing out into their knee. THIS IS NOT A KICK but rather must be a push.

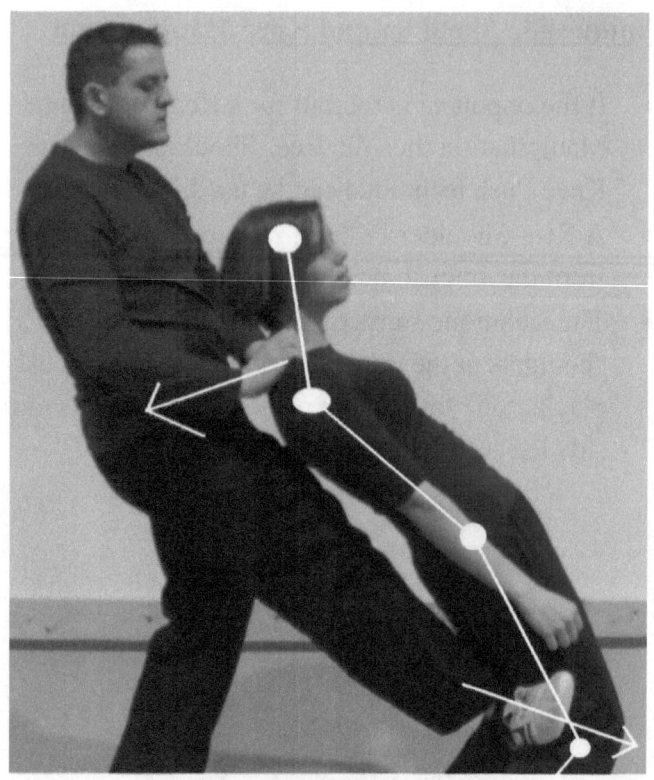

- Finish the technique by flaring their elbows up and to the side while pushing down forcing the subject to land on their back. Remember "head to heels" and push straight down not back into you.
- Take into account space requirements and decide whether or not to stay still, step sideways or straight back while the subject is falling.

Technique #4. Leg Reap and Sidewalk Slam

- The outside leg reap goes by many different names in traditional martial arts. In the Japanese arts it's most commonly referred to as O'Soto Gari. By

pressing the hips instead of the leg it becomes O'Soto Nage.
- From standing in front of the opponent grasp one arm (elbow or wrist) with your hand and use it to lift their arm up and out to the side.

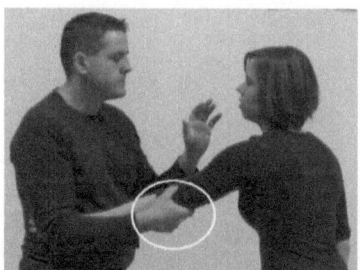

- Step beside them still facing opposite directions.
- With your free hand press their jaw up and away from you. Be careful not to insert your fingers near their mouth or else they might bite you.

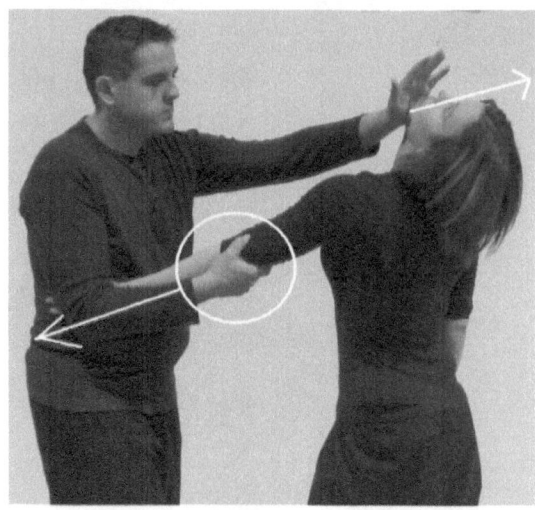

- As you push their head up and back use your leg closest to their leg to kick violently rearwards, extending their leg out in front of them.

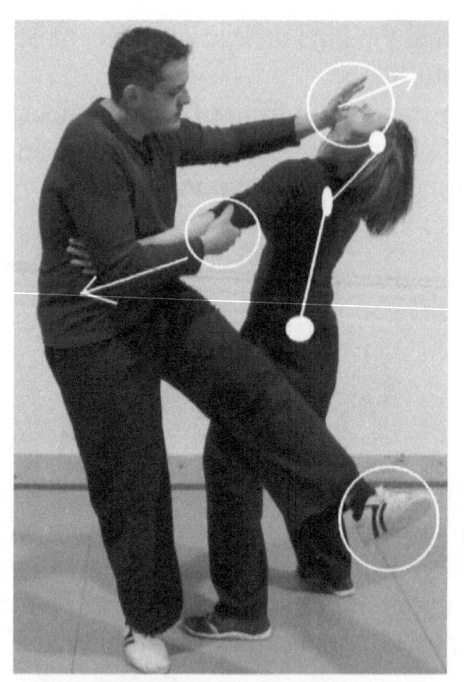
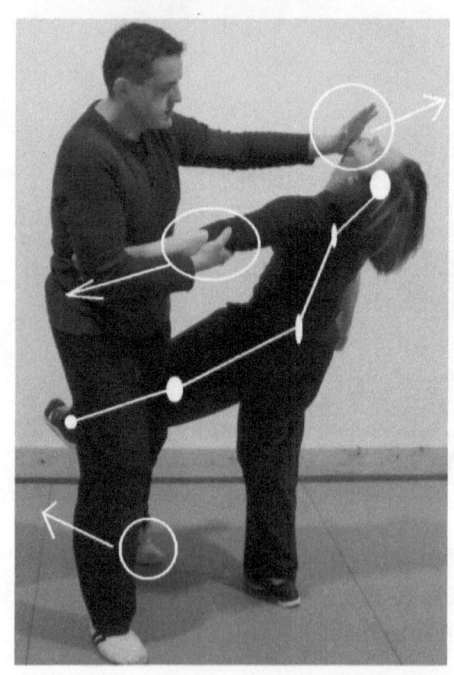

- To finish drop your center of gravity and draw down on their captured arm.

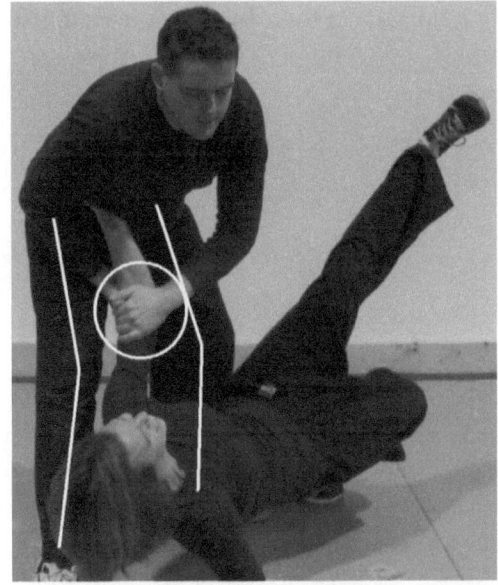

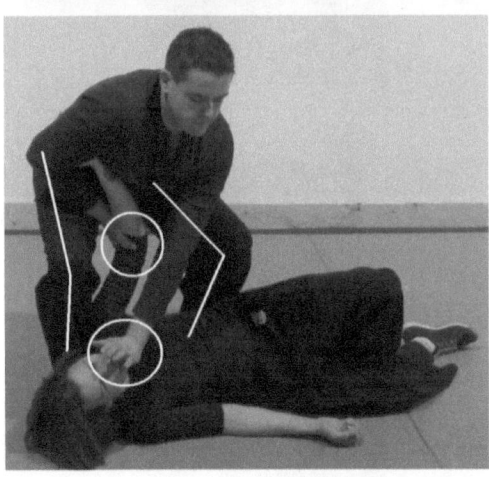

- To perform the Sidewalk Slam enter as before but this time as you push up and back on the opponent's jaw insert your hips under theirs and lift up with explosive force. If executed properly this will lift their feet off the ground by extending their hips and the jaw control will invert them horizontally so that they land flat on their back or on the back of their head.

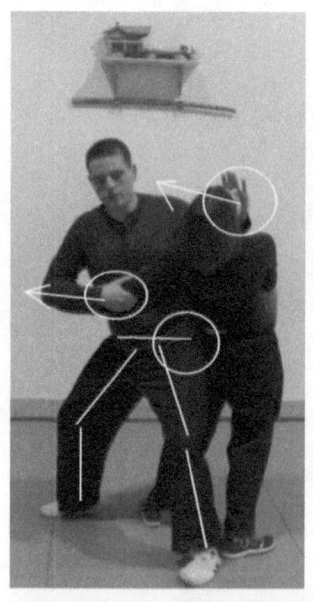

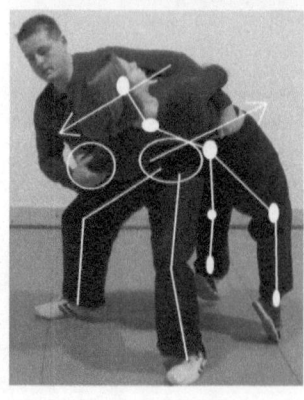

Technique #5. Turning Leg Reap

- The turning leg reap is also executed from standing in front of an opponent. In Bujinkan martial arts it is referred to as Ganseki Nage. Learning to move like this is excellent training to develop hip throws, primarily Seo Nage from Judo.
- The turning leg reap is a much more advanced throw because it requires several movements to be done simultaneously.
- From standing in front of your opponent reach out and capture a mirror side grab on their arm with 1 hand (wrist or elbow).
- Insert your opposite foot between their toes and turn by stepping out with your other foot. You should now be standing in balance with 1 hand holding the opponent's arm drawing it across your body with your opposite foot between their feet, your body and feet facing the same direction as theirs.
- With your free hand wrap it under their free arm by inserting your elbow rearwards under their armpit and capturing their arm for leverage.

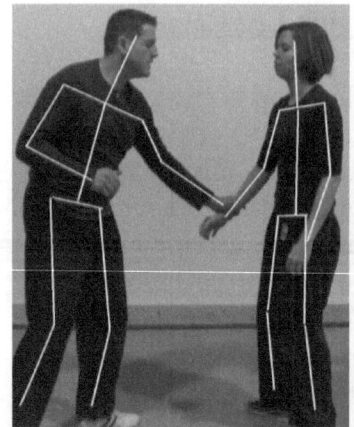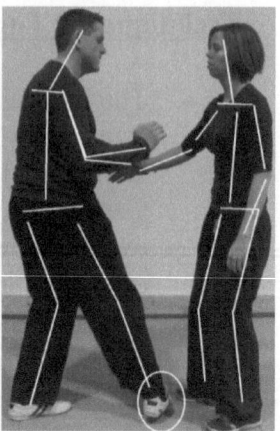

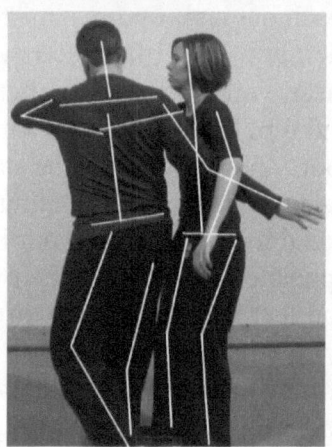

- Use this lever arm to press forwards driving their shoulders forwards as you kick out their leg rearwards to complete the scissoring energy requirement.
- Drop your center of gravity and draw on their captured arm across your body to complete the throw.

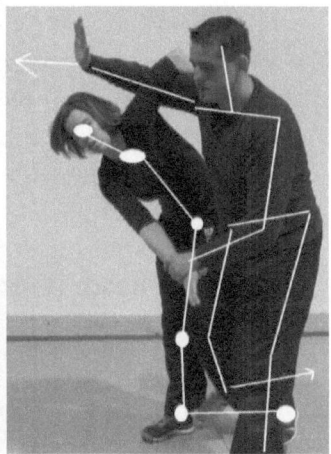
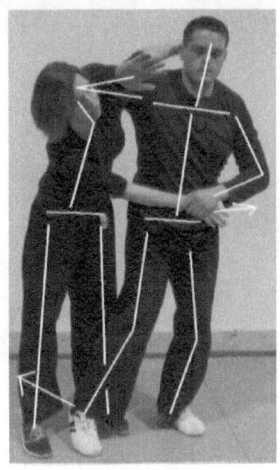

Technique #6. Pelvic Press

- A Pelvic Press is completed from the adversary's outside position. Start by standing beside your partner and just slightly behind them so their arm is in front of you.
- With your far arm grasp their wrist and pull it across your body to your far hip.

- With you close arm use your elbow to push up and back on their jaw.
- With your close leg use your knee and hip to push on the back of their knee and pelvis so that their lower body is moving forwards. Continue this motion to complete the scissoring component of the throw until their balance is taken and they fall.

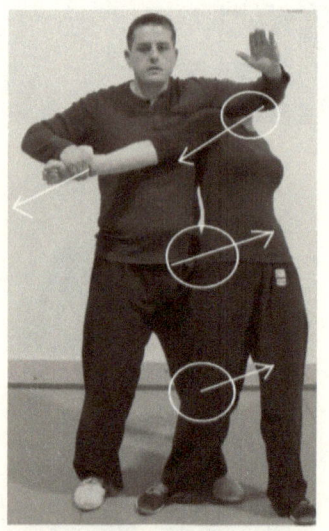

Technique #7. Windmill Takedown

- The windmill takedown is an advanced technique that requires particular attention to detail and footwork. It is often referred to as Ushiro Ganseki Nage in Japanese or puter kapala in Filipino Arts.
- From the inside position take control of the back of the opponent's head and pull down as you grasp their elbow and lift up. The best place to grip is at the base of the skull/top of the neck. The natural bony protrusions allow for a good grip at this location. Push until the other person is bent over at the waist.
- Complete the Windmill takedown by pulling up on their arm and pushing the subject's head under the arm. Make sure you move out of the way or else the subject will run into their legs perhaps initiating a new attack.

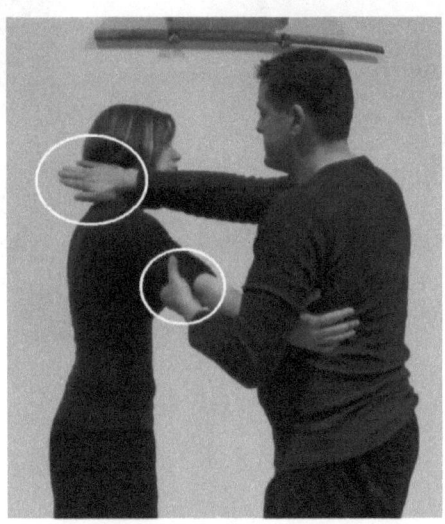

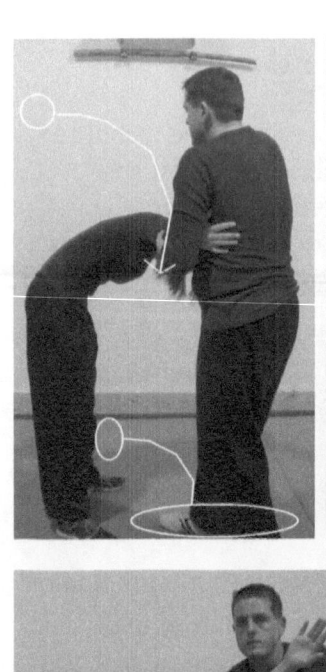
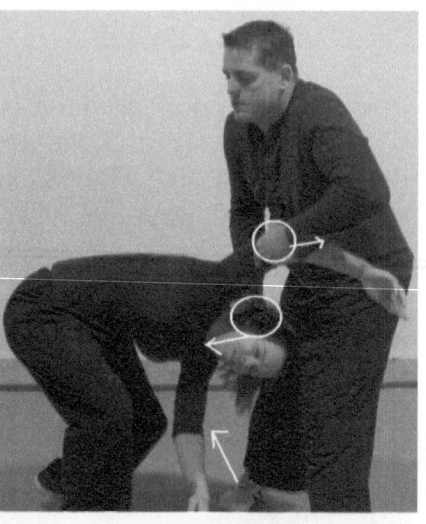

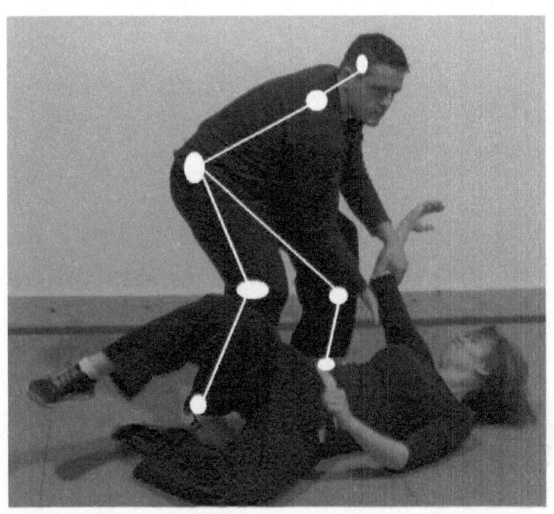

Balance Disruption Conclusion

The effectiveness of attempting to disrupt an opponent's balance is never guaranteed. People vary a great deal in terms of how well they maintain or recover balance. You should be comfortable flowing from one technique to another and executing techniques from a variety of situations and positions.

Balance Disruption techniques are generally completed as Goal #3, Finish the Fight. You must also remember there are several things to take into account before attempting to disrupt an assailant's balance such as the size and apparent strength and if you have the space to move in.

> **Flowing Through the Material**
>
> Once a basic comprehension of striking and skeletal balance manipulation are achieved it's time to put the pieces together. Remember when putting the material together to develop some techniques to save you in an altercation not to violate any level of the training model. The temptation can be to focus on a particular technique to force it to work with strength and power and break form. Remember that this violates *Natural Body Movement* and possibly *Tactics* and will leave you open to attack. Instead be patient and learn how to use that material properly.

Completing the Puzzle

In this chapter we're going to explore how Striking and Balance Disruption go together to complete Priorities 1-3 of an altercation. They were Don't Get Hit, Hit Back, and Finish the Fight.

Stopping the Initial Attack

- When being attacked it's important to stop the attackers weapon delivery systems from cycling. "Cycling" means applying force against you, retracting to a loaded position, and repeating.
- When intercepting an attack a 2-on-1 methodology is applied. This means both your arms intercept their 1 arm with a rigid frame.

- This frame pushes out from your core, but not so much that it causes you to break form or posture, with your elbows flexed slightly past 90 degrees.
- As the assailant attacks with a hook punch step into the attack and raise both arms.

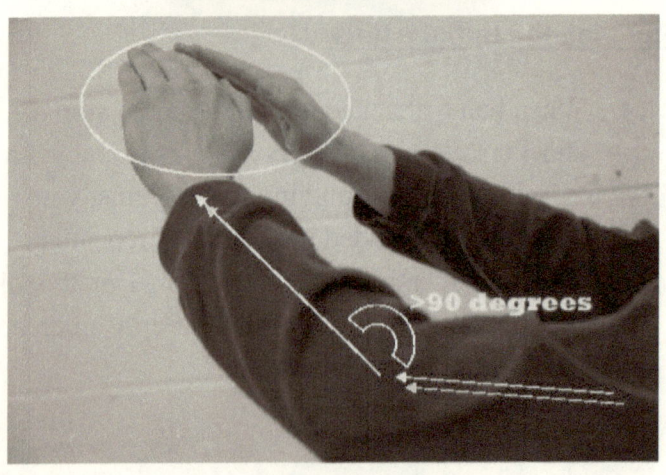

- Contact is made with the bony ridge of the hand or forearm. Fingers are cupped together for protection and contact is made on the forearm with one hand to stop the weapon from contacting the target and high into the bicep, shoulder, or chest to stop the forward momentum of the assailant.
- Once you have effectively stopped the initial impact of the weapon the second step is to stop that weapon from being able to cycle and attack again. To do this wrap their far arm over the attacking arm, pin the attackers hand into your armpit, and wrap your fingers around the base of the triceps digging into the bony protrusions where the radius and ulna connect to the humorous.

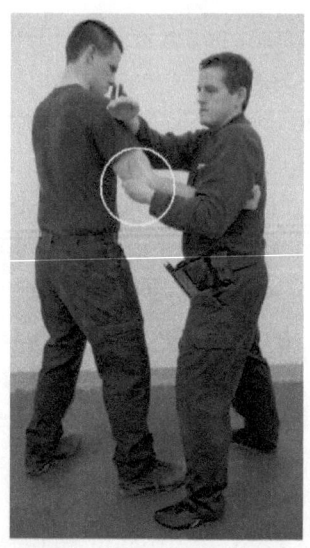

- Once the assailant's arm is effectively wrapped and controlled strikes are encouraged to interrupt the opponent's thought process. The best options are either an elbow strike to the side of the head or a hammer fist strike to the side of the jaw. In a lethal force situation eye rakes, throat strikes or grabs, and knee strikes to the groin are all effective options.

- Once control is established on the arm that attacked, your free arm applies upwards pressure into the jaw of the subject. Simultaneously draw down on the elbow with the grabbing hand and arm. This will force the subject's' eyes up and thereby break their balance to the rear. This position stops the subject from being able to effectively attack and allows you to drive in closer to the subject for the balance disruption techniques.

Applying the Takedown

- Where the assailant strikes with the corresponding foot forwards (i.e. right hand forwards with right foot forwards) it's quite easy to perform the *Leg Reap* or *Sidewalk Slam*.
- In the case where the opponent attacks "Boxer Style" the leg corresponding with their attacking arm may be rearwards. In this case reaching for the *Leg Reap* will likely put you off balance and prolong the encounter. Change techniques and utilize the *Windmill Takedown*.
- Compromise your assailant's base by kicking the inside of their far knee with the flat of the foot. By pointing the toes out you are able to maximize surface area and increase their chances of affecting the target in a dynamic confrontation.
- Once the subject's balance has been compromised complete the *Windmill Takedown*.

Transitioning Between Takedowns

- Variations of takedowns were included in Chapter 4 so that if an opponent defends an attempted technique you can hit them with one (or multiple) of the strikes from Chapter 3 and try a different technique. Learning to link techniques together is a very important part of training.
- Some of the possible combinations are illustrated. Remember though to use *strikes* to distract your opponent's thought process and thereby allow the opportunity for the skeletal manipulation and corresponding *balance displacement*.

- Each transition will begin from a *Leg Reap* attempt. In my opinion the *Leg Reap* is the #1 throw in your arsenal. It's easy to learn, easy to remember under stress, and highly effective. One other reason however is that it's likely that you'll be standing right in front of your opponent when the fight starts. It takes a higher degree of skill to obtain and maintain the outside position in a fight. By our nature we face each other when we fight.
- For the purposes of description assume that the initial attack came from the attackers right side and you've captured it with your left hook. Remember however that these skills should be practiced on both sides.

Transition #1. Leg Reap to Turning Leg Reap

- In this instance the opponent defends the initial *leg reap* attempt getting their leg out of the way. There are several ways this might happen but the most likely is that they step straight back with it putting it out of range of your sweep attempt.
- Now that the leg closest to you is out of range their leg furthest from you is forwards. This opens the opportunity for either the *Turning Leg Reap* OR the *Windmill*.

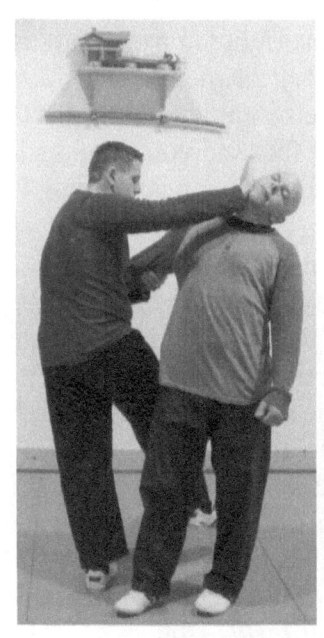 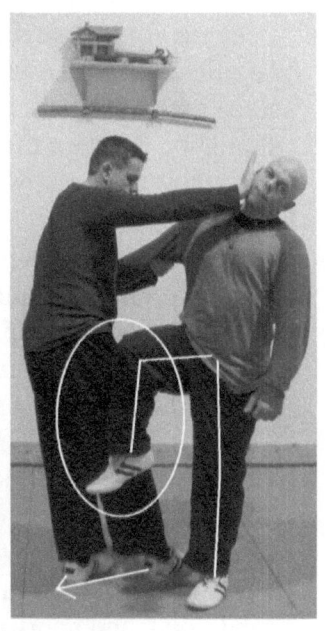

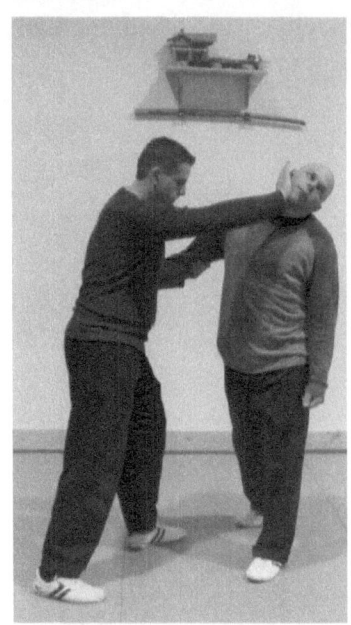

- Because you're using the right leg from both the *Leg Reap* and *Turning Leg Reap*, once the opponent steps rearwards with their right leg your right foot should be between their feet and you should still have their right elbow trapped and jaw pressed up and back.
- To begin the next technique a transition to the opponent's left is required. When you make this transition however we're going to lose the skeletal control from the jaw press. For this reason distraction strikes are needed to open the time frame for the transition. There are various combinations that can be used. I find a very effective option is to let my right hand slip off the opponent's jaw and as their head comes forwards apply an *Outside right elbow strike* to their jaw. From here drop your right hand down and apply an *Inside Hammer Fist* to their stomach as you simultaneously capture their arm with an under hook.

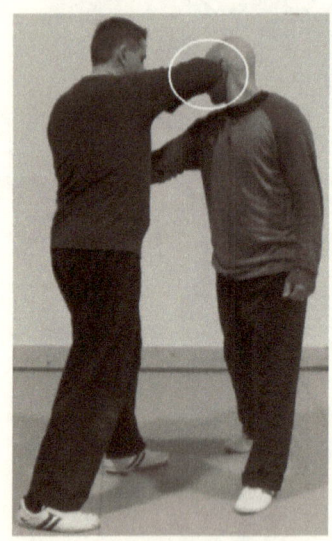

- From this position now apply the 180 degree turn to your left. Maintain your grip on their right elbow to draw their arm across your body compromising their balance from the waist. You should now be all the way over to their left side, their right arm trapped by the elbow in your left hand, your right arm wrapped under their left arm, facing the same direction as the opponent with your left foot between their feet.

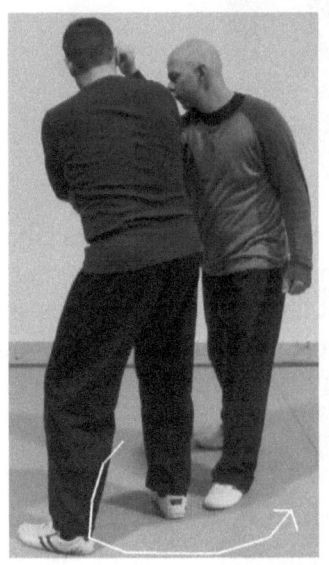
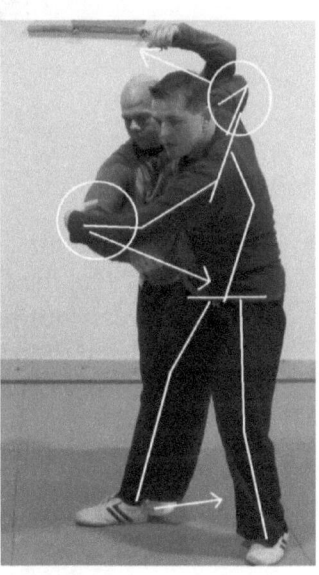

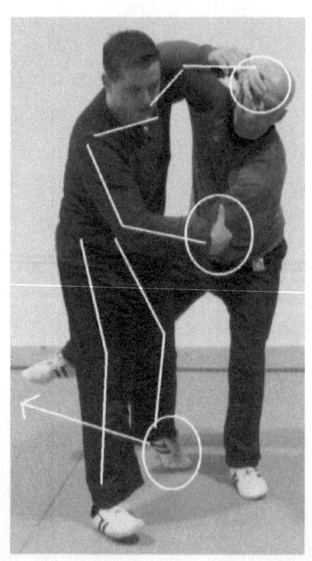

- If you practiced the *Turning Leg Reap* from Chapter 4 you know that the finish is simple. Slide your left leg rearwards, your left hand pushes forwards, and your right hand draws down on their elbow as you drop your center of gravity slightly.

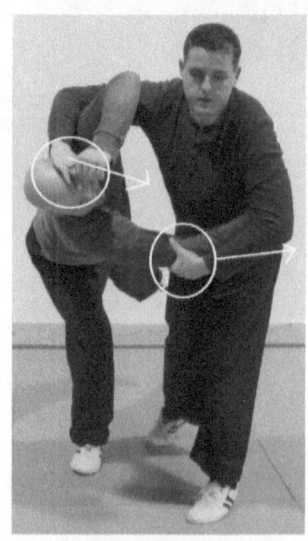

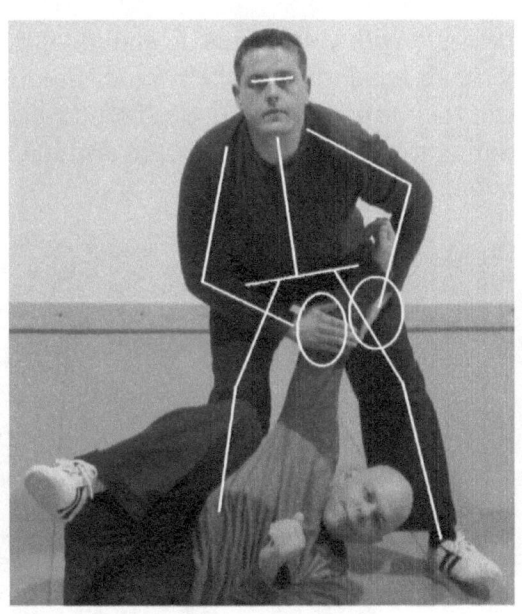

Transition #2. Leg Reap to Pelvic Press

- This transition illustrates 1 method for moving from in front of an opponent (i.e. in the Inside Position) to behind an opponent (i.e. the Outside Position). I'm going to use the *Pelvic Press* technique for the skeletal manipulation but from here it could also be the *Horizontal Rear Jaw Control* or the *Shoulder and Knee Manipulation.*
- Follow the first part of *Stopping the Initial Attack* previously outlined in this chapter. The transition starts from the point where you've trapped the opponent's arm, applied your strikes, and have obtained a jaw press.
- From here take your right hand off the opponent's jaw and insert it under their right arm. You should now have their right arm trapped in your left hand and your right hand under it. Loosen the grip with your left hand and lift up with both hands. Draw a

semicircle with your hands up and to your right to steer their hand towards their center line. Move under their arm as you do. So should finish standing to the right of their right arm in the *Outside Position*.

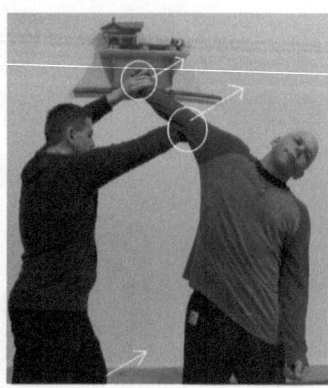

- If you turn 180 degrees right you'll finish standing beside them, facing the same direction as them. Now pull their right arm across your body in front of you.
- From here there are several striking combinations that work for a distraction. My personal preference is a *left straight punch* over their shoulder to the right side of their jaw followed up with a *rearwards*

left elbow that rises slightly under their chin. From here I hold the elbow in place for the pushing energy on the head and complete the *Pelvic Press Takedown*.

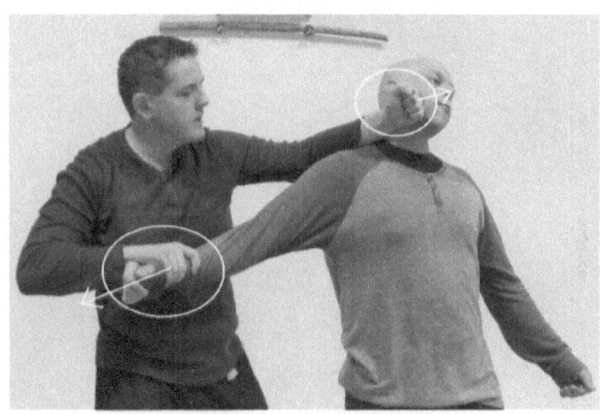

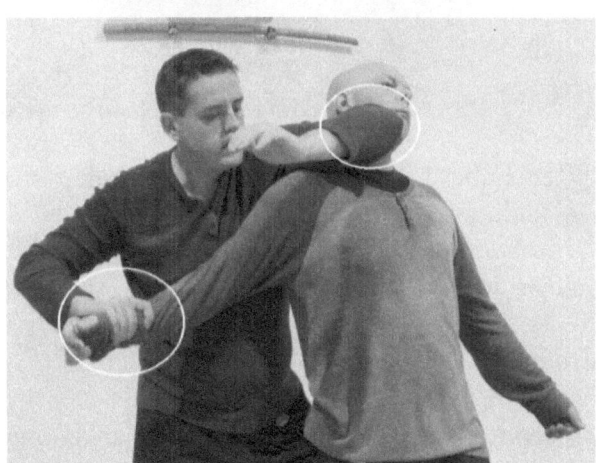

- Remember to practice both sides and also abandoning the arm and transitioning to the *Horizontal Rear Jaw Control* and the *Shoulder and Knee Manipulation*.

Transition #3. Leg Reap to Windmill

- Because the *Leg Reap* and *Windmill* takedowns are both completed from the *Inside Position* this is one of the less complex transitions.
- From a failed Leg Reap (see the beginning of *Leg Reap to Turning Leg Reap*) you need to release the jaw press with your right hand and stoop the opponent over at the waist. Again there are many different striking combinations that will allow to do

this but my personal preference is retract your right hand off their jaw and apply an *Inside Hammer Fist* strike to the right side of their jaw. From here clasp the back of their neck with your right fingers and pull down on the head as you apply a *Shin Kick* to the groin.
- Once your adversary is bent over at the waist apply the *Windmill* Takedown.
- Remember to practice both sides.

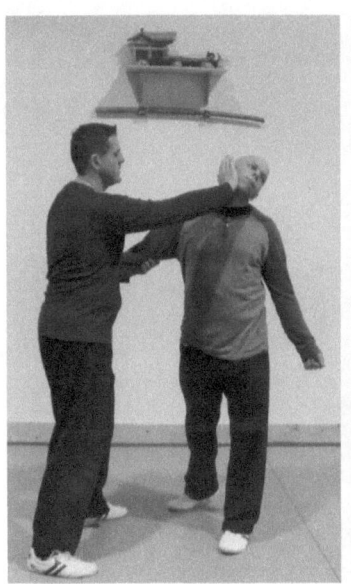 

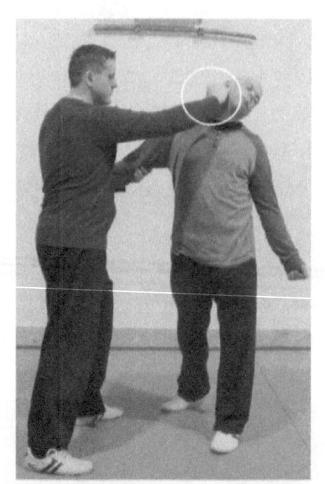
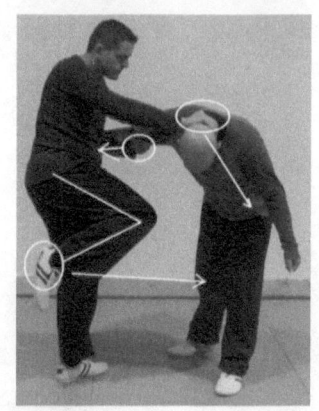
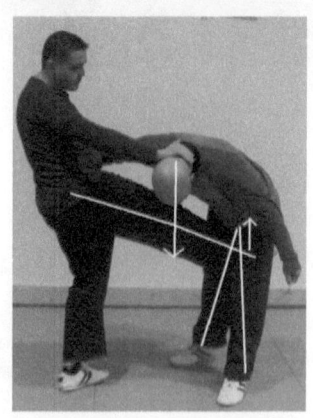

Completing the Puzzle Conclusion

The flow through techniques and counters in this chapter follow the basic flow in traditional martial arts such as Bujinkan, Filipino Martial Arts, and many forms of Kung Fu. This idea of closing the range with strikes and throwing your opponent to the ground has its roots in battlefield arts because once the opponent was on the ground it was easier to kill them with a weapon.

Now days this same methodology is applied to Combat Sport, particularly MMA. For the student interested in surviving a violent street encounter it is a very powerful set of *Tactics*. Once the opponent is on the ground it affords you the luxury of making a decision on how to precede. Is this opponent or situation so dangerous that from here you continue to attack them while standing over them or is this your opportunity to get to Escape and Evade, Apply First Aid/Self Aid, and Call the Authorities (priorities 4-6)?

Expect that all of your techniques will fail. A fight is a game of human chess with possibly lethal consequences. It is not enough to be thinking about what technique you're attempting. Like a chess master you must be thinking about moves ahead. This way if your opponent defeats a technique or it fails for another reason you're already 1 step ahead and flowing right to the next attack before your opponent has time to recover and counter attack.

> **Percussion and Precision Weapons**
>
> **Knife and stick combatives is a reality of today's combative environment. In some jurisdictions martial artists must also ensure they have an understanding of firearms, both how to use them and defend against them.**
>
> For the purposes of discussion Percussion Weapons refer to stick fighting, and Precision Weapons will refer to edged weapons.

Understanding Edged Weapons

Before learning how to use and defeat edged weapons you must first be aware of the realities of these threats.

- Edged weapons damage on a cycle where the weapon is trusted out in either a stabbing motion or a slicing motion, pulled back, and repeated.
- Interrupting the cycle is critical to surviving an assault of this nature.
- Once the cycle is interrupted tactical superiority must be established through use of a takedown.
- Knives can damage tissue on the positive (thrusting) part of a cycle or the negative (pulling back) part of a cycle.
- Knives can cause harm and damage on many angles, they don't malfunction or run out of ammunition.
- Because of the close contact range of a knife attack it's very easy for the assailant to hit the target.

- Because of the speed of the cycles it's very difficult to interrupt them.
- Because of arm speed it's very difficult to grab a subject's hand or wrist during an assault.
- It's rare that people will die from a single knife wound. For this reason if struck with the knife you must continue to take decisive action to protect yourself.
- The best strategy is to find cover, shielding, create space, or escape.
- Because most attackers will use an ambush tactic however it's nearly impossible to access a weapon before the assailant can begin to injure you with the knife.
- When using an edged weapon your priority should be to open gaping wound cavities and puncture organs that immediately shut down an attacker. Due to physiological changes during stress surface wounds may not bleed. Also certain organs can be wounded and won't result in stopping an attacker for up to several days. There have been accounts from American Prisons where inmates have received more than 100 puncture and slash wounds and not only survived but were still conscious and moving when they arrived at the infirmary.

Knife Posture

There has been an ongoing debate about the best way to hold and posture with a knife. Some of the points of this debate have been:

Forward grip vs. reverse grip
Weapon foot forwards vs. weapon foot rearwards
Knife visible vs. knife concealed
Saber grip vs. hammer grip

The posture that I use can be described as weapon foot forwards, weapon hand attached to hip, support hand raised protecting throat and heart, tip pointed at opponent.

I prefer my weapon side forwards so that I can hollow out my core thereby keeping my vital organs away from an opponent and still am able to reach parts of their body. My knife hand is kept close to my body to make it difficult for my opponent to grab it or otherwise attack it. It's visible as a deterrent to the attacker. Remember that according to the Ethics requirement in my material the best way to stop an attacker is without physically harming them. In every encounter it's my hope that by my posture and presence the attacker leaves if I'm unable to escape.

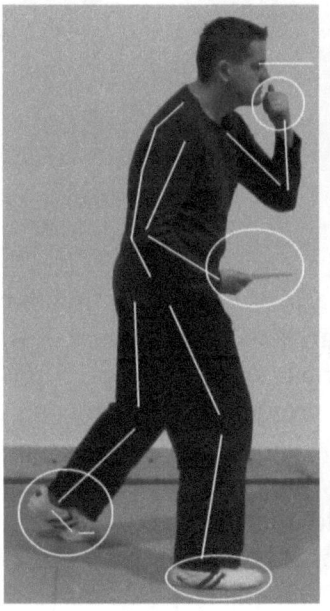 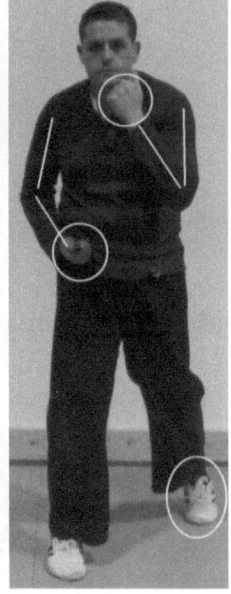

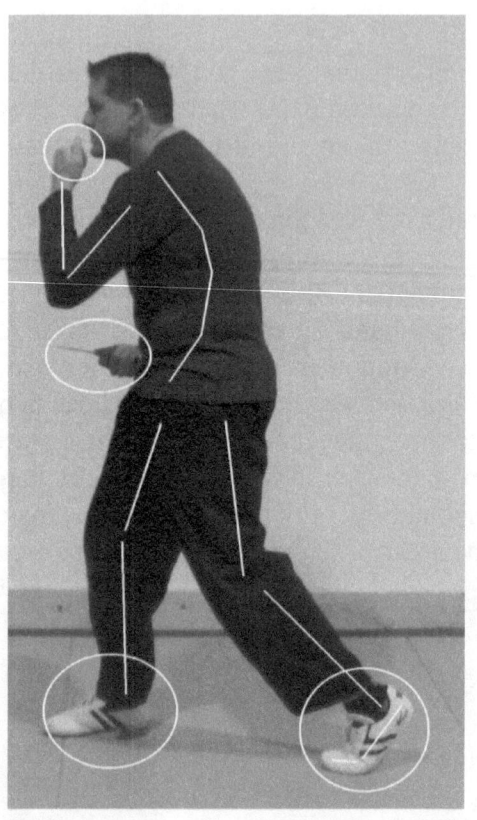

The saber grip is utilized so that my thumb provides counter pressure to keep my hand from sliding down the blade if I hit bone on a thrust. Also the saber grip is slightly more relaxed and provides better hand and wrist movement. The butt of the handle rests in the meaty part of my palm at the base of my pinky finger. I also train reverse grip but it's for rapid deployment of a fixed blade. When accessing a pocket knife or given the choice I use a saber grip.

It's interesting to note here also that in Japanese and Filipino knife arts the forward grip is favored. Some Japanese Koryo martial artists debate this point because in many Tanto Jutsu (knife arts) kata and techniques the reverse (Kage) grip is used. The Tori in the kata uses this grip because most of the kata's were developed to repel an ambush attack in close quarters and when they accessed the knife out of the obi they didn't have time to switch grips to a forward (Hi) grip. The Uke in the kata's however regularly thrusts with a forward grip to penetrate the organs and keep as much range as possible. This illustrates that given the luxury of time and preparation the forward grip was favored and the reverse grip was only used as an emergency in cases where there wasn't enough time to switch to the forward grip.

Cycling the Knife

I use a back cutting principle which means my hand and arm cycle the knife out to the target (positive phase) and apply the cut in the back stroke (negative phase) as the knife comes back to my starting posture. This is because I place a large emphasis on weapon retention. Using this manner of cutting helps to ensure that there's not temptation to reach for a target and compromise your own posture or fall into traps and baits by the opponent.

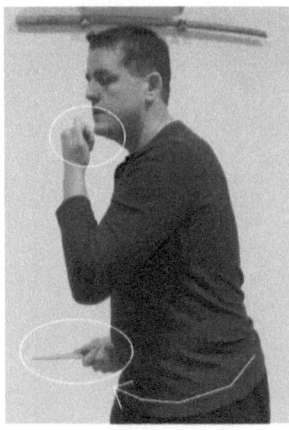
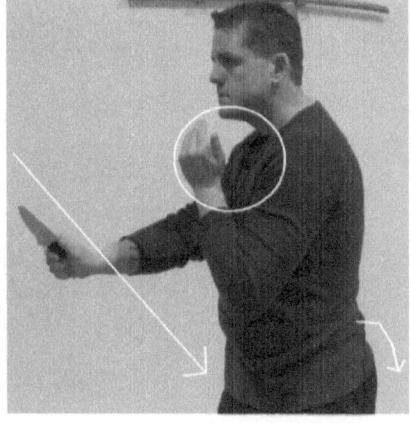

Targeting

Knives are effective weapons because they can cause tissue damage to anything that gets in their way. The emphasis however should be ending and altercation quickly. There is a misconception that hacking and slashing or just thrusting with the knife will do that. In multiple case studies however, most of them from prisons, people have survived over 100 thrust and/or slash wounds.

This isn't to say that the purpose of fighting with a knife is to kill someone. Rather it's to stop someone from hurting you (remember our foundational ethic!). Surface wounds and deep tissue wounds to the digestive system won't accomplish that. Attempting to thrust the heart and lungs is very difficult because they're protected by the rib cage and sternum.

For this reason I favor 3 targets. The first is the eyes. Even a shallow scratch to the eyes can stop a fight much less a deep slash or thrust. The second target is the throat. Some people think that the blood vessels on the side of the neck (carotid artery and jugular vein) are a good target but unless both sides are being opened it's not. The brain can continue to function with 1 side severed and the body's natural response is to decrease blood pressure on the side that's wounded to decrease blood loss and maintain blood pressure to the brain. This means that the best target in the neck is the wind pipe. Even a light impact to the windpipe makes most people gag and makes it difficult for them to continue fighting.

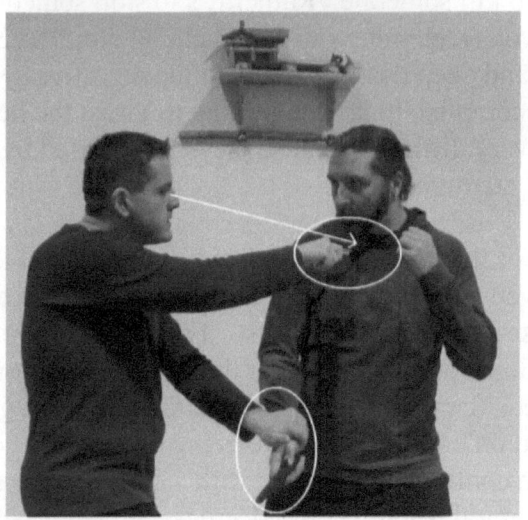

    The third and final target I aim for is the assailant's hands. Particularly their dominant hand if I know which hand it is. Impact to the hand can lacerate muscle and tendon and break the small bones of the fingers making it difficult for them to use their hands to form a fist, grab, or hold onto weapons.

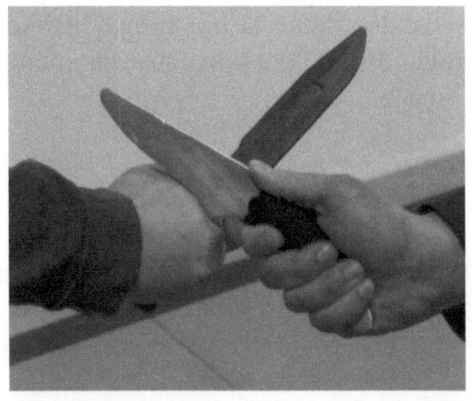

Stopping an Assailant's Knife

In a worst-case scenario the assailant will ambush and you won't have time to arm yourself. If this happens it's very important to maintain forwards pressure into the opponent to cut off their space. The most dangerous range to be in during an edged weapon encounter is what's referred to as the medium range. The medium range is an arm's reach away from the assailant.

The medium range is the most dangerous range because the assailant can cycle the weapon without having to move their feet. If you can't escape it's tactically superior to move into the close range (less than an arm's reach) and get control of the weapon arm at the elbow.

Once the assailant's arm is trapped strike them and take them down. From here you can either continue to engage OR escape.

Understanding Percussion Weapons

Before learning how to use and defeat percussion weapons you must first be aware of the realities of these threats.

- Percussion weapons only effectively deal damage on the positive phase of a cycle.
- Interrupting the cycle is critical to surviving an assault of this nature.
- Once the cycle is interrupted tactical superiority must be established through use of a takedown.
- Sticks don't open wounds but rather crush tissue under the surface.
- Sticks can cause harm and damage on many angles they do not malfunction and they do not run out of ammunition.
- Sticks require more space than knives to cycle.
- Because of the speed of the cycles it's very difficult to interrupt them.
- Because of arm speed it's very difficult to grab a subject's hand or wrist during an assault.
- It's rare that people will die from a single strike with a blunt object. For this reason if struck in the altercation you must continue to take decisive action to protect yourself.
- The best strategy is to find cover, shielding, create space, or escape.
- Because most attackers will use an ambush tactic however it's nearly impossible to access a weapon

before the assailant can begin to injure you with their weapon.
- When using a percussion weapon your priority should be to smash the head or hands.

Stick Posture

The posture that I use can be described as weapon foot forwards, weapon hand holds the stick so that just about ½ of an inch sticks out below my grip, support hand raised protecting throat and heart, and the stick resting on my dominant shoulder butt pointed at opponent.

I prefer my weapon side forwards so that I can hollow out my core thereby keeping my vital organs away from an opponent and still am able to reach parts of their body. My stick hand is kept close to my body to make it difficult for my opponent to grab it or otherwise attack it. My elbows are tight to protect the body and make them harder to hit.

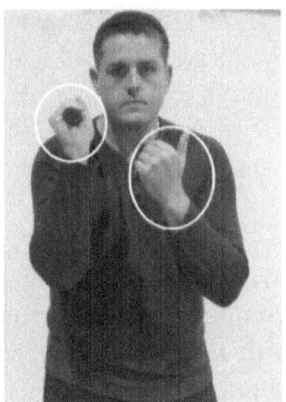

Cycling the Stick

Using the stick is slightly different than using the knife. Where the knife cuts as it's retained to posture the stick causes damage on impact in the positive phase of the cycle. I actually aim with the butt of the stick while it's resting on my shoulder. I squeeze my grip and rotate my wrist to start the attack. My shoulder falls into the strike as my feet push my hip and body rotation.

Unlike some systems my stick doesn't slash through the target. Instead it strikes out to where I want to attempt to hit and stops. If I hit my target it sticks to push the kinetic energy through the surface deep inside the target to cause internal damage.

Whether I hit the target or not the stick cycles back to retention posture immediately after the attack phase is completed. I either rotate my wrist to cross my weapon arm across my body, stick resting on my support arm shoulder butt aimed at opponent (closed posture), or I pull it back to where I started (open posture).

Targeting

While the knife will open wounds and cause some damage anywhere on the body in either the positive or negative phase of a cycle the stick will not. Remember too it's my goal to end this fight quickly for my safety and for my assailant's safety.

I only target the head or hands with a stick. I attack the assailant's head to cause unconsciousness or to stun the opponent. My secondary goal is to break their hand so that they can't use it to attack me.

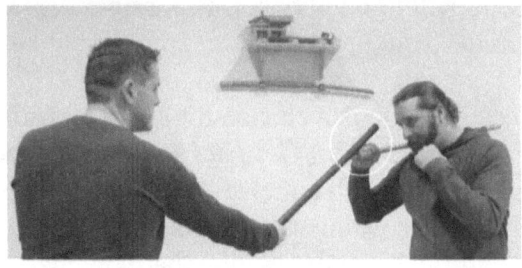

Stopping an Assailant's Stick

Just like when dealing with a knife attack if you're ambushed and can't access a weapon of your own or escape the best course of action is to attack the assailant and get into the close range. A knife and a stick are both examples of melee weapons and the strategy and tactics for dealing with them are the same. Once you're in the close range grab the assailant's arm at the elbow and begin striking them. As soon as possible use skeletal manipulation to take them down. From here you can either continue to engage or escape.

Precision and Percussion Weapons Conclusion

A weapon assault is one of the most serious threats you could face. It takes very little skill for the subject to be deadly with a knife or stick but a high degree of skill for you to protect yourself in contact range. Remember priority number 1, Don't Get Hit. While it's unlikely that a single wound will kill a person it is possible. A slash or puncture to the head, face, neck, or spine could be fatal.

Because there is a chance for a single wound to kill your first priority is *Don't Get Hit*. Some of the tactics you can use when faced with a melee weapon to not get hit are increasing distance, using shielding and cover, or escaping. If you have to fight it is imperative that you interrupt the attack from cycling and then takes the subject down to gain a positional advantage. The goal through training with these weapons isn't just to be able to use them but to be as efficient as possible with them and to understand how they work, the limitations of melee weapons, and how to defend against them.

Ground Fighting

In an encounter a Ground Fight can be an extremely dangerous thing. You must understand the importance of understanding how to defend against a takedown attempt. If the confrontation goes to the ground it is imperative to understand the positions and corresponding transitions that will allow you mobility and opportunity to fight back and protect yourself.

Understanding the Ground Fight Scenario

A ground fight is seen first and foremost as a violent dangerous assault. The reasons are:

1. In a ground fight situation more kinetic energy is delivered from strikes due to the nature of stomping and kicking and the fact that counter pressure increases the transfer of kinetic energy into the target.
2. In a ground fight situation whoever maintains the top position can generate more power and use less energy by striking with gravity and body mechanics.
3. The person on the bottom position quiet often can't reach the person with the top position with strikes due to body mechanics
4. In a ground fight situation you will likely be limited as to what weapons you can access to control the subject.
5. Assailant's generally become more violent once a fight hits the ground.
6. The person on the bottom position doesn't have the option of disengagement.

7. Moving on the ground requires more energy to overcome friction.
8. Your ability to deal with multiple opponent's is drastically limited while on the ground.

For the reasons listed above you must train mentally and physically to treat a ground fight assault as a dangerous situation that requires immediate action. The program is broken into 3 categories; preventing the take down, defending against a standing opponent and grappling with a grounded opponent.

Technique 1. Sprawl and Matador

- As an opponent attempts a tackle shoot hips back.
- Forearms simultaneously strike the opponent's shoulders and press into the opponent's jaw.
- Push off opponent to stay standing and adjust angle to opponent.
- Remember to illustrate that the primary control is from **JAW CONTROL**, not the actual sprawl of the hips.

Technique #2. Sprawl to Back Control

- As opponent attempts a tackle shoot hips back.
- Forearms simultaneously strike the opponent's shoulders and press into the opponent's jaw.
- Shoot hips back.
- Forearms simultaneously strike the supra scapular nerve motor point.
- "Ride" opponent to the ground and move to back mount position.

Technique #3. 1 leg trap release

- From a failed sprawl the opponent might manage to wrap up 1 leg.
- Strike down on back of the head with hammer fist or elbow strikes and pushes down on the back of the assailant's head while dropping your body weight.

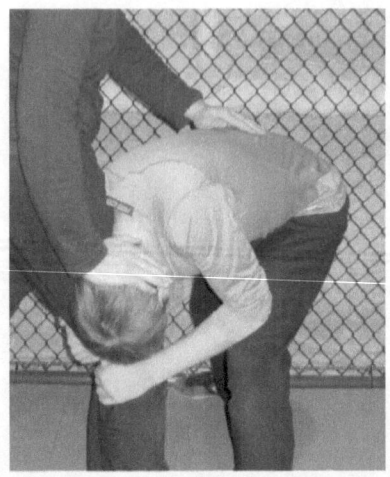

- Shoot your hand down along your body and leg between your body and opponent's head.

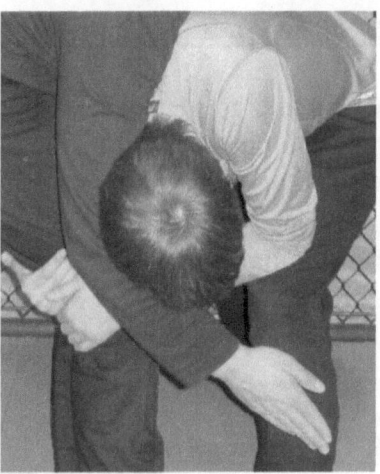

- Curl your arm up over opponent's face to begin jaw manipulation.

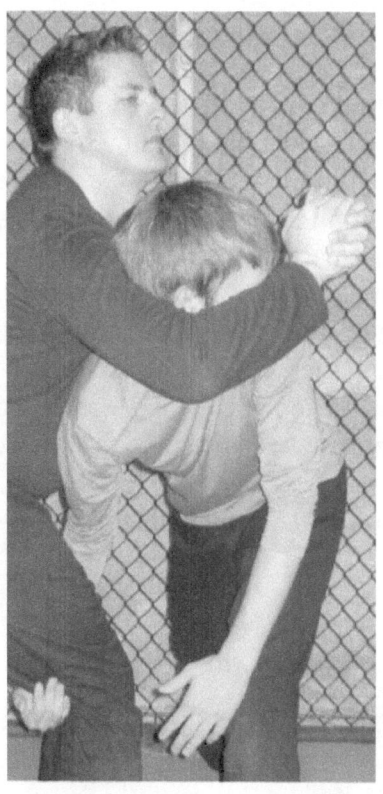

- Clasp your hands together and utilize a step and body twist to complete jaw manipulation takedown.

Technique #4. Back ground fight position

- If you find yourself knocked down to the ground and your assailant is standing over you use the Back Ground Fight Position to maximize safety.
- The position is maintained by staying flat on the flat of your back with one foot tucked in close to you on the ground and the other foot raised slightly.
- From here you can use the foot on the ground to move and the other foot to kick the assailant.
- You can switch your feet depending on what direction you have to move to stay facing your assailant.
- Keep your hands and head up.

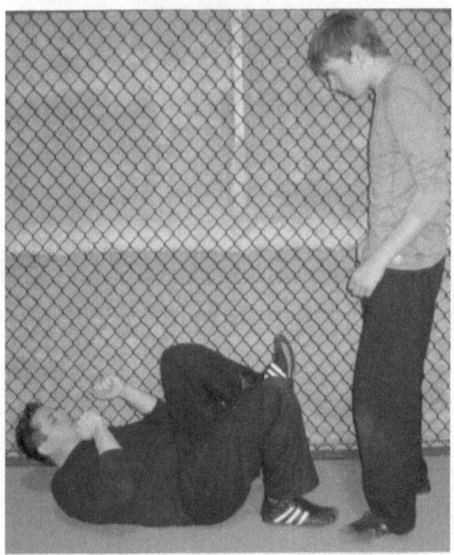

- When you deliver a low kick to your opponent's' shins there's a high degree of likelihood it will bring the opponent's head down to waist level. Your next kick can be a high kick to opponent's face.

- Various angles and targets including face, groin, shins, top of foot, and mid section can be struck.
- When the opportunity presents itself you can use a standing sweep to manipulate the assailant's balance and take them down. One example is the knee bar takedown.
- To complete a knee bar takedown roll onto your side. Use your low leg to hook the back of the assailant's' foot with your toes. Pull their foot towards you as you place your high foot just below their knee. With that foot push forwards to lock the

opponent's knee turning their leg into a lever and taking them down.

Technique #5. Shrimping

- Lift the hips to clear your body off the ground, push off the ground with the balls of the feet and simultaneously shoot hips back and reach for the feet.

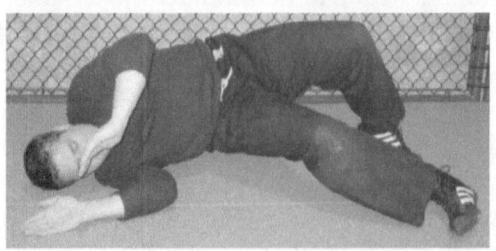

- When an opponent is in your guard Shrimping can be used to create space. After creating space insert a shin and knee to create the corner and keep the subject away from you.
- Once you create space you can adopt the Back Ground Fight Position and engage with kicks.

Technique #6. Getting back to standing from the ground

- Shrimping is also used for getting up off the ground.

- After Shrimping use an arm post to establish 3 point kneeling posture.
- Be sure to keep your eyes and hands up.

- From 3 point kneeling posture standing up using a calf raise to transfer pressure from the knee to the ankle and shift your hips forwards slightly to relieve some of the pressure in the legs.

Technique #7. Bridging when subject on full mount

- If the assailant gets on your Mount it is very dangerous for you. They can use body mechanics to strike down into your head and face but you cannot effectively strike upwards at them.
- It is imperative to force the assailant to use their hands to maintain their balance instead of striking

you. Grabbing their arms is ineffective because they can generate enough movement and strength to break your grip.
- Use your knee to drive straight up into the base of their spine to shift their weight forwards and force them to put their hands down on the ground.

- Once your assailant's' hands are on the ground trap one of their ankles with the back of one of your legs and grab their elbow.
- To complete the bridge raise your hips off the ground as high as possible by pushing off the ground with the balls of your feet.
- Once your hips are off the ground look over one of your shoulders to set an angle and roll to that side.
- You can use jaw control to assist.

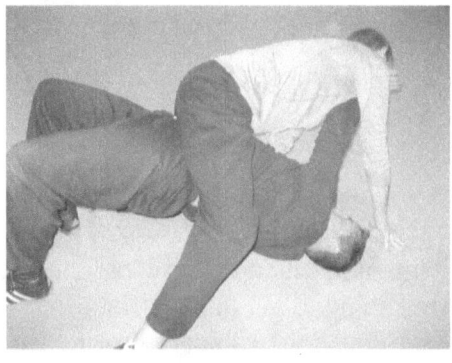

Technique #8. Scissor sweep when subject in guard

- In some instances when an assailant is in your guard it's difficult or impossible to use Shrimping to create space. In these circumstances using the legs to pull the subject deep into the guard makes it so that they can't create the space necessary to accelerate a strike. You can't hold a subject indefinitely in guard however. Particularly in the case of multiple opponent's.

- To pull guard wrap the legs around the subject just above their hips and sit up to grab them. The best way to grab with the hands is on the back of the subject's head and their right elbow. Pull them into your core and hold them there to prevent being struck.

- When you detect an opening reverse the position using the Scissor Kick.
- While maintaining an elbow trap the open the guard and shrimping to get one leg flat to the ground. Use this leg to push the subject's posting leg from the knee using either the back of your leg or foot.

- Use your opposite leg to push into the assailant's' ribs and rolling over your low leg.
- The technique is called the Scissor Sweep because your legs should cross each other through the assailant's' body.
- When completed properly you can roll all the way over and on top of the assailant's mount.

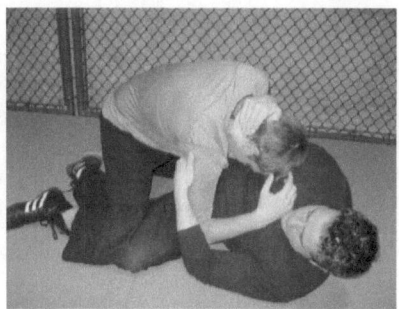

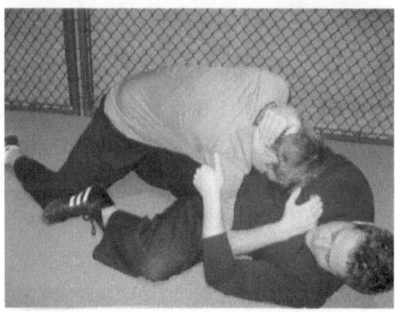

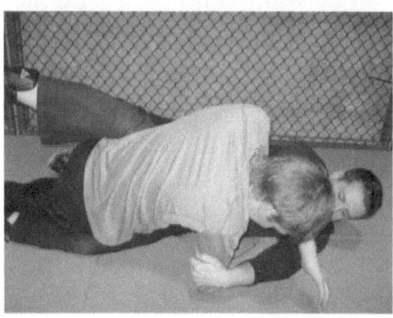

Technique #9. Scissor Kick Reversal when subject on rear mount

- The first priority when an opponent is on the Rear Mount is to protect the back of the head from strikes and the neck from a choke. This is done by shrugging the shoulders and clasping the back of the head with both hands.

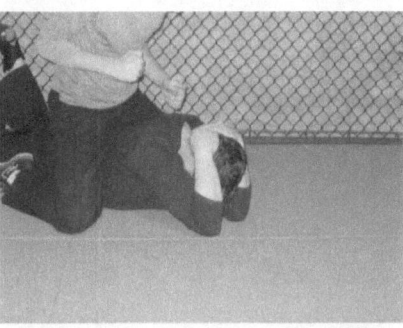

- Immediately after protecting the back of the head and neck you should use the Scissor Kick Escape and scramble with jaw pressure to side control.
- This is done by digging the hips into the ground so that the subject can't wrap their legs around and hold on and violently scissor kicking the legs, one over and one under the other, to rotate the hips.
- If the subject falls onto their side then reach up and use jaw control to push their head away as they scramble to the side.
- Once side control is established you can continue to engage or escape.
- If there is space between you and the adversary during the Scissor Kick then you might roll under them and finish with the subject on your Mount. From here use the Bridge.

Technique #10. Scrambling when in Guard

- In the case of being trapped in the assailant's Guard, the Guard Break can be used. First however base and control must be established. This is accomplished by using jaw control to sit back seat to heels, posture high with knees wide to control base and hands to subject's stomach.

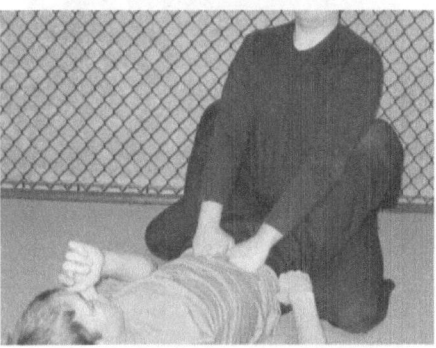

- Next walk your knee over to line up with subject's' tail bone and re establish base with other knee under subject's leg. This in combination with elbow pressure into the inner thigh and strikes will eventually open the subject's guard. Be sure to keep your other hand up to protect your head and neck.

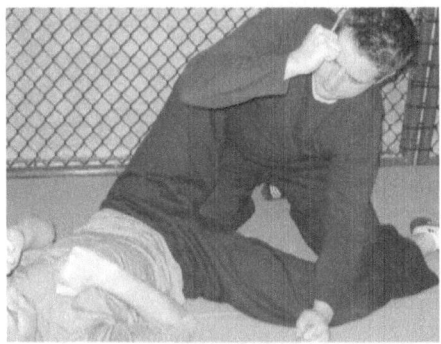

- Once the guard is open bring the far knee over the subject's' leg to pin it to the ground and prevent them from wrapping a leg with theirs.

- From this position the other leg can be brought out and side control can be established. If you decide to continue to engage then the knee on belly method of getting on the mount can be used.

<u>Technique #11. Break-dancer Reversal when in a North-South Headlock</u>

- North-South occurs when you and the adversary are facing each other. This term can refer to many different positions in which this can happen. This is most likely to occur when both parties are on their knees and the subject either wraps your neck for a headlock or wraps around your body.

- From this position you must utilize angles. To do this first decide which side you're going to attempt to escape on. This is generally decided by which side of the opponent's' body your head is pressed against.
- Once this is decided use an arm to control the assailant's' hands and, in the case of a headlock, looks into the subject's ribs. Next the posture up on the far knee and arm and begins establishing their escape angle by opening their leg on the side they're going to escape to.

- Next bring the far leg through the opening they created and pressures back into the opponent's' ribs with the back of your head while simultaneously sitting onto their buttock.

- From this position you can continue to engage by scissoring your legs and maintaining back pressure into the subject. They will either end on side control (if the opponent landed supine) or on back mount (if the assailant landed prone).

<u>Technique #12. Back Door Escapes</u>

- In certain situations you can't move the other person. In these situations a transition method known as "Back Door Escape" is utilized. The concept of the back door escape can be utilized from any position where the assailant is on top and you are supine.

- To utilize the Back Door Escape from a failed bridge maintain hip elevation and inserting one arm below the opponent's' inner thigh.

- Use the inserted arm to create pressure over your head as hips fall back into the space and legs pull you out from under the opponent. Turn to face your adversary and adopt the Back Ground Fight Position.

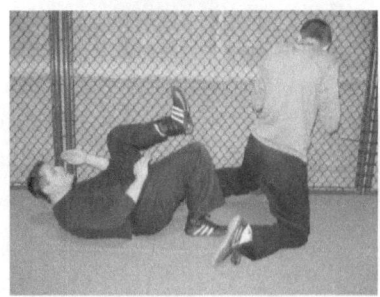

Technique #13. Twisting arm control when on Mount

- Once full mount is established Twisting Arm control is the preferred method to establish a position. First use strikes for encourage your opponent to cover their head and face. Use two-on-one arm control to angle their arm across their own jaw.

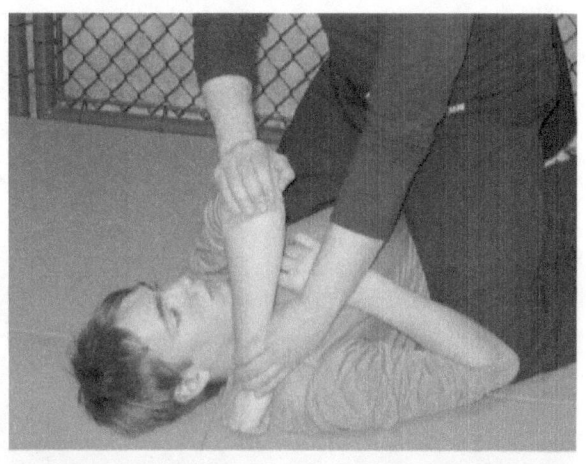

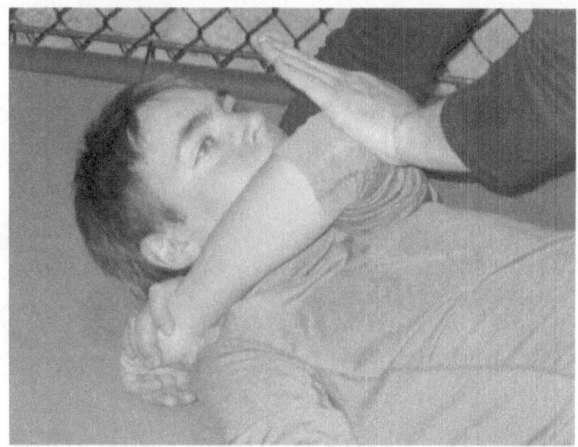

- Use body control to keep the arm in place over the jaw while reaching behind the head with one hand and grasping their wrist.
- Posture to a 3 point posture while pulling up on the subject's' wrist with arm behind their head and push down on their elbow with your other hand.
  Remember that power comes from the hips.

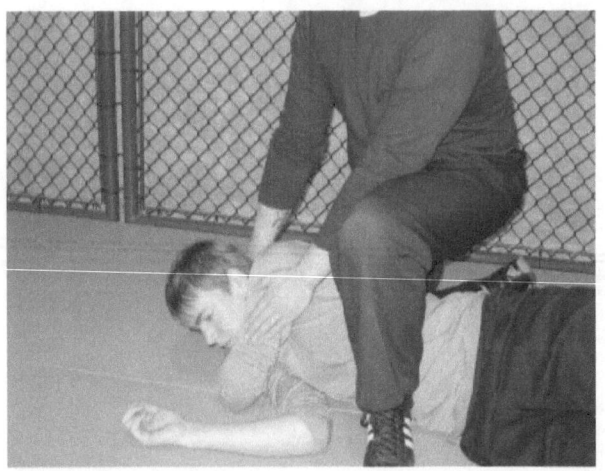

- Establish rear mount.

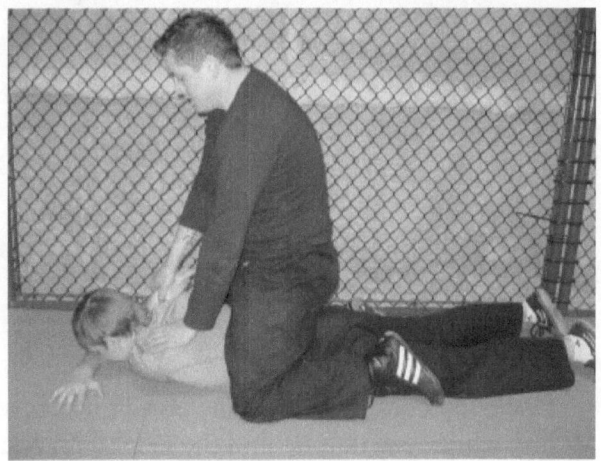

Conclusion

In a violent altercation you are usually responding to a sudden attack and often don't even know the nature of the attack. Ground fights are very violent and dangerous confrontations. Therefore you must be comfortable responding, moving, and transitioning on the ground.

Articles of Interest

I taught my first martial arts class in the spring of 1999 for my college Recreational Activities class. I knew right away that it was something I would want to do for the rest of my life.

Shortly after receiving my Shodan (Black Belt) in Bujinkan Budo Taijutsu I started running a small martial arts class. I realized early on that teaching was a big step of my personal growth. I also realized that there weren't enough hours in a week's worth of training to transmit everything to my students that I wanted to get across.

For these reasons, as well as self and club promotion, I started writing. Attached in this chapter are the articles I've written over the last 7 years. Some of them focus on police combatives, some of them purely on martial arts, and some of them on health and wellness. Where possible I've attached the date the article appeared and where. Writing these articles was a big step in my personal development and I hope you'll see an evolution in them as you make your way through them.

12 Tips to Implement A New Paradigm in Your "Defensive" Tactics Program
April 2008
W.I.N. : Critical Issues in Leading and Training Vol.1

As I travel to different courses and seminars I see a common thread amongst warrior trainers, lack of training. On countless occasions I've met trainers from different departments across the world that've been thrust into their position and not been adequately prepared. When this occurs one of the most serious consequences is that recruits don't get the training they need and can subsequently be set up for failure. Often these trainers have no idea that they're not equipping their officers with the tools necessary to be successful. Many administrators, coaches, and trainers may truly believe that they are providing the most desirable training, and are likely honest hard workers themselves. So what then can we do to fix this problem?

The problem may be with the defensive tactics program itself. Many of these programs are designed with the wrong mindset in place. This mindset follows the trainers and in turn is passed onto the officers whose lives they touch. So just what is the "wrong" mindset? What exactly is wrong with many of our current "Defensive Tactics" programs?

The problem starts with the word "Defensive." What is "defensive" about police work? Officers "defend" the public by "Controlling" the offenders, subject's, and situations. This idea of being "defensive" starts right at the outset of these training programs and then saturates the training all the way through. From the outset officers are taught to defend themselves in an altercation, not to control the situation, control the persons involved, and utilize violence, power, and explosivity to their advantage. Allow me to demonstrate my point with some illustrations.

In a current training program in the US trainers wanted to implement force on force scenario training. In order to implement the training without injuring recruits or quarries they placed two lines on the floor two meters apart from each other. Quarries aren't permitted to cross their line, and likewise with the recruits. This means that if a recruit decides that it's appropriate to respond with baton strikes he has to strike the air to simulate that use of force.

In this instance what is the recruit learning? How to strike air. Some trainers might make the argument that they're learning how to recognize a particular subject category and make a decision to respond. Can't this be done through the use of video?

Again from our brothers in the US, one state standard for recruits is 16 hours Defensive Tactics training. Six of these 16 hours must be classroom base. Again I ask you, what are these recruits being taught? Remember this is a State standard for every police agency. This means that every officer in that particular state is only receiving 10 mandatory hours of Physical Defensive Tactics training.

A Provincial Sheriffs Department in Canada completely changed its Defensive Tactics program. The amount of training was doubled. Officers were taught to think offensively and to be the predator in any altercation. Force on force simulation training was implemented. However the firearms program remained the same as it always had been where officers are taught to qualify rather then to gunfight. Officers spend all the time on the range shooting with one eye closed in order to score their shots at up to 15 yards. There is no movement to cover or support hand shooting covered. There is no marker cartridge scenario training. After over a year of being implemented the firearms training still hasn't been changed and now many of the elements of the DT program have begun to revert to the way they were.

These are just three examples of the current state of Defensive Tactics Training for many agencies. Very few agencies have made their way past this type of training to truly equip officers with the skills they need to save their lives when necessary. So the question begs to be asked, what can we do about it??? Below I've offered 12 suggestions to the trainer officer to ensure their brothers and sisters of the shield receive the knowledge, skills, and mindset required to be successful in a law enforcement career.

Stop using the word "Defensive." Starting immediately, if you haven't already done so, draft a proposal to your agency heads to change the name of your program to "Control Tactics." Why the name change? This simple little thing sends the message to every recruit that they are expected to take control of subject's and situations, not defend themselves. When people hear the word "Control" it conjures an image of officers taking the initiative in confrontations to control the subject, witnesses, crowd, and any other element of the confrontation.

Stop using the phrase "Officer Survival." This over used little phrase conjures images of officers getting their asses kicked, but it's ok because they survived. In this line of work survival is not enough. Replace such phrases with "winning." Officers should be encouraged to think like a predator. Not in terms of seeking the weak prey but in terms of training like a predator, practicing skills, utilizing small unit (i.e. pack) tactics, utilizing weapons and sensitive targets, and, when appropriate, striking with ferocity until the threat is neutralized. Phrases like "Winning Mind," "Predator Mentality," "Warrior Spirit," and "Ferocity of Action," tell trainees that it's ok to use violence to hurt someone to control them, that it's appropriate to initiate the use of force once a determination about a subject is reached. These phrases tell the recruit that it's only acceptable to win an altercation, and that survival is a by-product of winning, not the other way around.

Your control tactics program should be no less then 80 hours in length and should include handcuffing techniques, empty hand fighting, ground fighting, empty hand lethal force/CQC, intermediate weapons, firearms retention, joint manipulation, pressure points, and takedowns. As well there should be a minimum of 4 hours force on force simulation training including lethal force scenarios where recruits are permitted to make mistakes and then correct the mistake during the scenario, and another 4 hours of evaluation. Ultimately several days of Force-on-force training would be desirable but for agencies on a tight budget and time restraint no less then the eight suggested is acceptable. Eighty hours is enough time to include a class room element where video presentations and lectures are provided. As well firearms and control tactics should be merged so that instructors from each discipline are on the same page and teaching the same tactics, techniques, and mindset. Firearms training should focus on an actual gun fight and not qualifying. Most of the training should focus on winning a lethal force encounter and trainees should be educated in the physiology and psychology of combat. Any less than 80 hours isn't enough to cover all the elements of a program and do them justice.

Focus more on dynamic skills then static drills. Teach the officers how to apply the skills they've been taught in various and dynamic situations. This means that once officers have enough static drill to perform the technique with a minimum level of skill all the drills should be dynamic where officers are using their skills in simulated scenarios with their partners. This begins to move the officers' mind set away from skill based and begins to teach them how to apply their skills in a simulated application. Stress inoculation drills should be built into your training to teach the trainee how to perform the skill under a high level of emotional stress. This also recruits to experiment with fixes to a problem and learn transition drills to and from different force options.

Become goal orientated. Too many programs focus on the techniques of the program, not the goal it's designed to reach. This means that if your officers are able to apply the skills just enough to get the job done, then that's fine. This encourages your officers to improvise and problem solve on their own. Also consider implementing a 2 prong view to examinations. A written and practical exam can evaluate the basic skills and articulation and a second goal focuses force-on-force scenario exam can measure goal orientation.

Teach the principles of the technique. For example there are several different ways to manipulate the joints in human limbs to reach a desired result. When teaching joint manipulation for example, teach the officers why and how the technique works and how it can be modified for various situations. Once the recruit has the basic idea they can be provided some time to practice applying the technique in different situations and experiment with what works. This method of self-discover is usually a very powerful learning tool. This also encourages problem solving and goal orientation as opposed to skill base.

Learn from the lessons in the field. If a technique is never used in the field it's likely because the officers realize that other methods are more desirable for obtaining their goals. Evaluate your program regularly to determine if changes need to be made. Pay attention to incident reports, court room testimony, and any surveillance video. If things are happening out there that you're not training for, change your program. This needs to be a constant evaluation process. Perhaps techniques not being used can be modified to better suite the unique environment your officers operate in.

Stop telling officers what they will and won't do. The last I looked we were training adults. Adults in general, and especially law enforcement officers, will determine when and how to apply what they've learned. For this reason phrases like "Always do this..," or "Never do this..," are rarely appropriate. Encourage officers to think for themselves. You won't be in the field with them telling them when it's appropriate to make an exception to a generally accepted rule. What you can explain to them is where a particular response may fall in the scale of desirability and what the risks associated with different responses are.

Include an "emotional triumph" lesson. If we're already teaching trainees how to survive a confrontation, why not teach them how to survive burnout, hyper vigilance, and the day-to-day stress of the job. More officers become victims of suicide and substance abuse then are killed in the line-of-duty each year. This is generally referred to as "emotional survival" but we've already explored why we need to move away from that word. "Emotional triumph" or "emotional victory" may be more appropriate substitutes. This is an opportunity to educate officers about post traumatic stress, survival stress, stress management and post-retirement planning. There is excellent work available on the subject that trainers can implement into a 4 hour block and encourage their officers to follow up more on their own.

Change your PT program. Often trainers tell me the reason for their PT program is so that recruits will pass their exams at the end of training. While this is important is it really educating our officers? What happens once the recruit has completed training? If the change is made from PT to Phys Ed this puts an emphasis on teaching the officers how to maintain a healthy and active lifestyle for their entire career. Community resources can be researched and presented to the officers during training so that they know how to access programs after classes are completed. Also this gives the trainers an opportunity to impress upon the recruits how critical performance related physical training and diet are.

Include an off duty lesson plan. Depending on your jurisdiction this lesson will change drastically. Department policy, municipal, state, and federal law must all be taken into account when preparing this lesson plan. Weapon choices may change drastically. If officers are permitted to arm themselves with a side arm off duty then it should be encouraged that the same, or similar, side arm as their on duty weapon be used. Officers must be provided some direction as to what's expected when off duty and when not to get involved in an incident. If officers aren't permitted to be armed with a sidearm then edged weapons and/or martial arts weapons (i.e. Cane and mini-stick) might be their only option. Recruits must be taught what's expected off duty and be encouraged to make good decisions. Also family action planning can be presented to the officers to help them in case of an off-duty incident.

Realize that you're teaching for the recruits, not for yourself. Our role as trainers is to provide our brother and sister officers with the skills and knowledge necessary to work safe and stay safe, and in return keep the public safe. This is your primary focus, public safety. For this reason you must realize that most recruits are like sponges and want the trainer to answer every question for them. Instead encourage the officers to challenge what's being taught, think of creative alternatives, and answer questions for themselves. Constantly evaluate the program you deliver and your skills as a trainer, and don't be afraid to admit when you've discovered a more desirable way of doing things and encourage change. Your mission is a difficult and challenging one. When the public need help they look to peace and police officers. When those officers need help they'll be looking to their trainers. As a trainer you may constantly find yourself in the situation where management and administration aren't supportive of your initiatives. Find ways to deliver the best program you can and constantly educate your administration until you have the support you need. Always remember it is your mission to educate your officers. You never know when the training you provided may influence someone's life. It may be the lesson you taught that saves and officer, or the lesson you didn't teach that kills them.

These 12 simple suggestions can help to modify any current Defensive Tactics program. Some of these suggestions may seem radical and unorthodox but I encourage you to ask yourself, is it time for a paradigm shift in my current DT program? If the answer is yes then I hope these suggestions find you and your officers well and provide the vehicle for positive change in your agency.

Training the Mind Part I: Self Talk
July 2008
Punch Magazine

In the business of hypnotherapy and motivational speaking one of the most critical aspects is the notion of "self talk." Self Talk is simply the dialogue we have to ourselves about ourselves in the privacy of our own minds. Below I'm going to list a few options for your consideration to improve your training and martial ability.

1. Developing the Winning Mind. This idea is widely used by police officers and professional warriors. Brian Willis of Winning Mind Training shares this philosophy with hundreds of officers from around the world. One of the most important dialogues we as martial artists have with ourselves is surrounding the conclusion of a confrontation. Many martial artists use the term "survival" to define what their goal is in a confrontation. Brian Willis suggests using the term "Winning" to define your goal in a confrontation. There is a big difference between the two. It is possible to survive a physical confrontation but let it destroy you emotionally and mentally in the long run. It is also possible to survive an altercation but suffer a serious injury in the process. If we focus on winning, however, we begin to prepare ourselves to perform in the most desirable manner during the confrontation and prepare ourselves for the emotional rollercoaster that follow's.

2. Developing Affirmation Statements. Take a honest evaluation of your skills and determine some short term goals. For example your goal might be "I want to develop my hip toss." Now turn that goal into an "Affirmation Statement." Simply rephrase the goal to "I am skilled in my ability to perform the hip toss," or even more powerful, "I have a strong and powerful hip toss." These affirmation statements process a powerful image of success in the subconscious mind that can help lead to success.

3. Stop Visualizing. Not all people are visual learners. For this reason stop "visualizing" your goals and begin "imagining them."

By changing our language from "visualize" to "imagine" it permits you to experience the mental drill in your own unique way instead of trying to force yourself to visualize it. If you do visualize whatever it is you're imagining then that's great. Not all people will have that experience though.

4. Imagery Drills. Once you've determined your goals begin using "Imagery Drills." Simply put imagine yourself achieving those goals and performing them. High level athletes have been doing this for decades, if not longer, and attribute their success to it. Simply imagine the goal or skill being performed perfectly. This allows a martial artist to train constantly in their own mind.

5. Eliminate Negative Self Talk. Are you your own worst critic? Do you constantly put yourself down regarding your skills and abilities? Every time you do this your subconscious mind imagines a negative sequence of events and becomes programmed for failure. If you talk to yourself though the way you do to your friends you will pick yourself up and begin programming your mind for success. Consider this, "If your friends talked to you the way you talk to yourself, how long would they remain your friends?"

    Whether training for recreation, competitive sport, or combat, these 5 simple suggestions can help you begin to program your mind for success. In any activity in life being mentally prepared is just as important as being physically prepared. Compare how many hours a week you spend preparing your body compared with how many hours a week you spend training your mind. Like training the body, mental training is an active exercise that takes time, resources, patience, and dedication. There are several resources and professionals that can provide more detailed direction. These 5 suggestions will help you begin preparing mentally for success.

What are you doing to make a difference?
Fall 2008
Monthly Student Newsletter

As fall starts to turn to winter I'm always grateful for the wonderful life I have. As I look around and see people less fortunate than myself I can't help but imagine what they must be experiencing. It's during these times I ask myself, "What am I doing to make a difference?"

This is especially true as we near November 11, Remembrance Day. As we remember the 45,000 Canadian troops who gave the ultimate sacrifice in that conflict for our freedoms ask yourself, "what can I do to make the world a better place."

One suggestion is to go through all your old clothes and find ones you don't wear anymore for donation. There are several charities including churches, Salvation Thrift Stores, the Mustard Seed, and drop in shelters that need those clothes for those less fortunate.

Another suggestion is to volunteer at a local seniors lodge or residential facility. An icy sidewalk in the winter can make it very dangerous for those seniors to leave their residence. Shoveling sidewalks in the winter for seniors can allow them the freedom to enjoy the outdoors without fear of injury.

A third suggestion is make a cash donation. Several charities could use cash. Pick one you identify with and contribute. Just make sure you do your research first to make sure your money is being spent on what you intend for it to be spent on.

Make sure you thank a war vet. Even if you don't agree with the conflict they fought in realize that those warriors fight those battles so that you and I won't have to. Please make sure you attend a Remembrance Day Service this year and thank the men and women who sacrifice to protect our homes and freedoms.

      These are just some suggestions and some of the things I do to put positive energy out into the world and make a difference for those less fortunate than myself. Please take time this fall to do something to make a difference. Then I challenge you to make it a daily thought. Holding the door open for someone, offering someone help, taking the time to listen to a friend, these are all things we can do every day to make our world a more positive place. Remember that you reap what you sew!

Living the Christmas Spirit as a martial artist
December 2008
Monthly Student Newsletter

What exactly is the Christmas Spirit? Depending on your religious or spiritual beliefs it may be a celebration of the birth of Christ. However this holiday is celebrated by many people regardless of their religious beliefs. So than what exactly is so special about this one holiday?

It's my belief that the Spirit of Christmas is much more than a celebration for one religion. I see Christmas as a celebration of love for the entire world and everything in it. To some of you this may sound a little farfetched or too "touchy feely." But remember a true warrior does what he does out of love, not hate. Allow me to elaborate further.

Traditional Ninja from Japan believed that what they were doing had a positive effect on the universe by eliminating or controlling evil or violent men. Even when carrying out assassinations they believed they were making the world a better place. They trained and fought out of love for their family, their community, their nation, and for the entire universe. This is really what Ninpo is all about. Fighting out of love, not hate. Still not convinced? How about Samurai? Why did they fight? Out of love for their emperor, their family, and their nation.

Examples can be illustrated from throughout history. The story about Leonidas and his 300 Spartans at the battle of Thermopoly. These 300 warriors surely knew they were marching to their death. But they understood their sacrifice was necessary to protect their families, their friends' families, and their nation. They fought not out of hate for their enemy, but out of love for their home.

Take the opportunity this Christmas to re-connect with your commitment to fight for what you love and what you believe in. Take some time during this busy season to remember what Christmas is all about. It's not about greed or presents. It's about celebrating what we have, who we are, what we believe in, and the love for ourselves, our friends, our families, our beliefs, and for our very world and all the good things in it. Take some time this Christmas to renew your vow as a warrior to fight the good fight and make the commitment to fight not out of hate for your enemies but rather out of love for all the good things in your life.

Please also take a moment to thank a warrior who can't be home with their family this Christmas. While we're enjoying the company of our loved ones, police, medics, fire fighters, and soldiers will all be away from theirs protecting us.

What have you done?
December 2008
Monthly Student Newsletter

Now that 2008 is over and 2009 is upon us it's an excellent opportunity to ask yourself this question, what have you done to make a difference? In the last 12 months what opportunities did you seize? Whose life did you make a difference in? If you were gone tomorrow would anyone notice?

When preparing for my new year these are questions I ask myself. What could I have done better? Where are the areas in my life I need to improve? What are my priorities? The biggest question I ask myself, after having attended some of Brian Willis' Winning Mind Seminars, what am I doing to live a legacy?

These are more than just New Year's resolutions. These are hard questions to answer. They force us to look deep inside and decide if we like who we see there. These questions aren't meant to just be asked at New Years, but rather a constant evaluation at our lives as warriors. What are we doing to live the warrior spirit?

This includes our physical training, mental conditioning, and how we conduct ourselves every day. This is the path of the warrior. I've often said anyone can become a fighter, but only special people become warriors. It is a constant quest. One that should be evaluated daily to see if you're still on the path.

I was blessed in 2008 with some awesome opportunities. I was privileged to meet new people, attend some fabulous classes and seminars, and really be inspired by some true warriors. I have no idea what the 2009 will bring, what challenges I will face. But I can vow to continue on my own journey down the warriors path. To live my life with passion and energy. To strive to make every day better than the one before. To seize everyday as a celebration of my life. To live my legacy every moment.

I encourage all of you to do this same self-exploration exercise. Ask those hard questions with honesty. Evaluate where you want to make real change. Talk to someone else about it and tell them what your plans are. This forces you to take ownership of your plan and holds you accountable to someone else. Remember, this is more than just a New Years resolution; this is a recommitment to the warrior lifestyle and a chance to renew your passions.

I'd like to thank everyone for a great 2008, and sincerely wish you all the best in 2009.

Predator vs. Scavenger
January 2009
(never published/presented)

Introduction

Recently during a woman's' self defense course I was using a popular analogy and imagery concept where you take the student through an exercise to convince them to begin thinking like a predator. This exercise is quite well used in the police training community and basically comprises of using images that people associate with predator animals to describe aspects of themselves. The goal of the exercise is encourage students to see themselves as the predator in a life or death situation. Most warrior trainers that I known conclude the exercise by then describing the students enemies as predators to drive the point home that the enemy such a confrontation is a dangerous animal and uses the same tactics and weapons as the "good guys." Industry leaders such as Lt. Col. Dave Grossman, Brian Willis, Coach Bob Lindsey, Phil Messina, and Joe Truncale use this analogy just to name a few.

While leading the women in the class through the exercise it was my intent to finish the exercise the same way these other warrior trainers do. For some reason though I used the term "scavenger" to describe the enemy. I was so full of passion it wasn't a conscious decision, just an image that came to me while describing the brutal murder of an innocent woman that had recently occurred in my city. I did notice though that the women in the group really grasped the analogy and it seemed to work well.

Then during the 2008 ILEETA conference I heard a lot of instructors talking about the concept of predator versus predator as it pertains to officers versus subject's. During a presentation I made I found myself once again full of passion and energy and describe the subject's as scavengers. Again I had an image in my head of a weasel type of animal scavenging around and trying to pick the easy meal.

I realize that great minds in the world of LEO training present the predator versus predator concept but I wonder if this idea of predator versus scavenger could also be effective and accomplish the same goals. Please allow me to explain further how I use the concept and perhaps, whether as a warrior or warrior trainer, you can use it to your own benefit as well.

The Imagery

For the first part of this discussion let me describe how I see the predator. This is the most important and critical part of the exercise. What's critically important in this exercise is the images and spirit of the discussion. Some of the animals I'll use to describe certain positive traits or warriors may also exhibit some scavenger behavior. There is no perfect predator in nature. There is no animal that has all of these traits, and there is no predator that doesn't exhibit some scavenger properties. Remember that this is an exercise in imagery, not biology.

The first thing I think of when I think predator is pride. Predator animals always seem to have a sense of self worth and pride about them. Think of a tiger for example. How do you imagine that animal in your own imagination? Is he walking tall and proud or is he bent over and lame? Is he clean or filthy? If he is dirty is it because he is too lazy to clean himself or is it the kind of dirt that is earned through hard work, toil, and battle? Even though scientifically speaking these animals don't have a since of self, how do you imagine them? That's more important than the literary biological explanation.

The second image that comes to mind for me is power. Power is a by product of strength, speed, and explosive or ferocious action. In Canada, where I'm from, there's a ferocious animal named the Wolverine. When I think of strength, power, speed, and ferocious action this is the animal I think of. Imagine a large badger if you don't know what a wolverine looks like, and imagine that animal attacking animals more then twice it's size with such power and ferocity that it's prey is completely overtaken. This small animal is known for such ferocity that it is the subject of many tales from the wild north. It is thought that a wolverine could, and would, stand its ground against a grizzly bear for its meal.

The third thing that comes to my mind is weapons. All predator animals use weapons to be successful in accomplishing their mission. Felines, canines, and bears, just to name a few, all have claws and powerful, sharp teeth. These natural weapons balance the playing field when they are attacked and defending their lives or when they're hunting for their very survival. There isn't a predator animal alive that doesn't use weapons to their advantage.

The fourth thought I have when imagining the word predator is tactics. Think of the wolf pack for a moment. Imagine the pack hunting game. What tactics do they use? Attacking during low light hours, using camouflage and ambush tactics, and the use of small unit tactics to confuse, exhaust, trap and overwhelm their target. It's these tactics that make a wolf pack so feared, much more so then a lone wolf hunting on his own.

The fifth image that comes to my mind is social behavior. Predators that remain in groups have a social behavior that is accepted and known by all members of the group. A rank structure exists and movement up through rank is gained by being the strongest and wisest of the group. Negative behavior is not tolerated and the offender is often subject to a punishment. Think of a troop or apes. There is a very strong social order and the troop works together for the benefit of each individual and for the good of the whole. This social code is so strong that members of the same species will rarely kill each other in a contest of skills.

The sixth and final image I have when I think of the word predator is training. All predators engage in play at a young age to learn their arts. Think of bear cubs for a moment. Imagine them rolling and biting and wrestling with each other. This is how they learn to fight and learn their combative arts that will serve them as adults.

For the second part of this imagery drill let's explore some of the images of a scavenger. Remember that this is an exercise in imagery, not biology. There is no perfect scavenger and many share traits with predators. Many predators in the wild will scavenge when their lives are at stake and they happen across an easy meal. What's important here however is how we imagine these animals and the traits, or lack of certain traits, that defines the term "scavenger" for us.

First the scavenger doesn't look like a proud animal. They often are dirty looking and look defeated. Their shoulders slumped, eyes looking around nervously, and their head hung low. Think of a rat. Not a very proud image comes to mind does it?

Second is the lack of power and strength. Compare an Eagle to a crow for example. The same power and strength isn't required when preying on the dead or dying as opposed to hunting for a meal.

Imagine the difference in tactics between a predator and a scavenger. Where a wolf pack will use group dynamics to over whelm its prey, a fox will sneak its way through the shadows into a hen house to steal eggs. Scavengers' still use camouflage, and some use small party tactics, there is defiantly a different image comes to mind. As opposed to a pack of wolves running down a stag imagine a trio of coyotes running down and cornering a frightened rabbit.

The final image I'd like to share with you when I think about a scavenger is that of a carrion eater. Somebody who reaps the fruits of other people's hard work and labour. Imagine a group of vultures around a kill that a pride of lions has made. The lioness' stalk and fight and bring down a cape buffalo much bigger and stronger than them. Now during their hard fought meal a group of vultures arrives to take advantage of someone else's hard work. Imagine those vultures as they tediously sneak in for a bit. What happens when the lioness gets up from her meal to chase them away? Do they stand their ground either alone or collectively? They run off with what little scrap they could steal.

Indeed the very word scavenger conjures certain images without even drawing specific examples from the animal kingdom. Close your eyes and think of that word for a moment. What images came to mind? Scavengers look like predators, they may even sometimes act like predators. They have teeth and claws. They may stalk alone or in groups. They use low light settings for movement and attack. They use camouflage and ambush to their advantage. They may even attack live game. But there's a certain spirit to the word. Something intangible that comes to mind when we think of the word scavenger.

When imagining the word predator often people see proud, strong, powerful hunters who use weapons and ferocity to overcome prey bigger and stronger then them and are capable of amazing physical feats. There's a certain essence to word predator.

In contrast to that when people are asked to imagine the word scavenger there's a much different image. Sneaky, weak, little creatures who are afraid and nervous and live their life in the shadows feeding off the weak, dead, or dying. There's a certain essence to the word scavenger.

Compare the different images that come to mind with the following, tiger, lion, wolf, eagle, bear, and wolverine, with those images that come to mind with the following, fox, coyote, raven, vulture, raccoon, and weasel.

Conclusion

Instead of using the traditional predator vs. predator analogy I prefer to use the predator vs. scavenger analogy. Our officers use similar physical and behavioral strategies as any other predator. They train from their induction into the tribe, just like cubs learn and are accepted into the pack. They use weapons to hunt and in defense to give them the edge. They use camouflage, ambush, and group tactics to be more efficient at their craft. There is no doubt that our officers should not only see themselves as predators but that they are indeed predators.

But what about the bad guys? Are they really predators? I prefer to see them as scavengers. This helps me to separate my mission from theirs. My mission is to hunt the scavenger, to rid the world of the dirty vermin. When I think in terms of predator and scavenger it helps me to distance myself from my enemy, to see him as something different then I am. It helps me to see him as something not as special as I am, as something not as proud or strong.

And what about the cowards who attack children and women to cripple our society and steal from us our most precious and loved resource? Is this any different then a scavenger who steals eggs from the nest when mom and dad are gone because he's too cowardly to face opponent's who might best him? How about cowards who steal from the elderly or sexually assault the young? Is this similar behavior to the scavenger who waits for the elderly prey that can't fight back or attack the cubs who are easy prey?

It's true that predators in the wild will take the easy prey during the hunt. One difference is what they hunt. Scavengers always steal, eat the dead and spoils of the predators kill, and will never attack anything that has a chance to defend itself. If we look at a lioness we can find examples of her attacking cape buffalo who outweigh her, are stronger then her, and who have weapons, to feed her young. Would a scavenger ever attempt anything like that? The scavenger might even eat its own young.

Another difference is when they're caught. A predator might face is captor; put their skills to the test, battle for what they believe is right and true and necessary. But the scavenger? He slinks back the fringes of society to hide in the shadows and find the next unguarded nest. He doesn't walk with his head high and proud, instead his head his down, his shame from being abandoned by the rest of society and tribe weighing heavy on him. Back to the edges of the tribe to fill his body with garbage to fill the hunger inside.

This can be seen time and again with the behavior of school shooters. Once the police arrive, the real predators, the scavenger can't face them. All they've practiced is their skill at stealing and sneaking and hiding. Not fighting, not testing themselves, not standing up for their way of life. When there's no physical escape, when they can't get back to the edges of society, back to their shadows, they take the final escape and end their own life. They don't challenge to predator to preserve their way of life. In one last move of desperation they escape the only way they can.

The last part of this presentation for officers to draw a clear distinction between us and the bad guys. If we see the bad guy as a predator he may be our equal. He may be as good as me. He may be able to best me.

But what if I see him as a scavenger? As the cowardly, dirty, garbage eater in the shadows waiting to steal what's precious to me if I leave it unguarded As the predator I hunt him relentlessly as he hides in the shadows afraid to face me, afraid to test me, afraid to put himself to the test. I won't lower my guard because there's the scavenger in the shadows sniffing around waiting to steal from me what's most precious and then run away back to the edge of society again where no one cares for him, where there's no pack, where there's no rank, no team, no love. Back to the shadows and garbage where he belongs.

The one risk of this analogy is that officers may not respect the abilities of the scavenger. When using this imagery drill as a warrior or warrior trainer the point must be driven home that the predators must respect the skills and methods of the scavenger. If the predator doesn't respect the methods of the scavenger and lowers his guard the scavenger will sneak in and rob them, steal from them, attack them. The most important part of the imagery and the analogy is convincing officers to see themselves as predators.

Great minds in the business of law enforcement support the predator on predator imagery and discussion to motivate officers to work hard, have confidence, and get out of a state of complacency and denial. I love the works presented and have used so much of other people's material to motivate myself and my students that I don't know where I'd be without the people who dedicate their lives to make a difference.

I just offer this new perspective as a slightly different way of looking at the same idea. Since thinking about it I have changed my view. Soldiers from foreign countries that meet our brave men and women on the battlefield are no doubt also predators. But terrorists who hide in holes in the ground and wait for us to drop our guard on the nest, in my view, are not.

I hope that this brief discussion about imagery and the analogy that I use can offer something else to think about and use when using the already powerful and accepted predator imagery.

Identifying the different types of martial arts
January 2009
Gateway Gazette

When exploring the different types of martial arts available it's important to be educated and be able to identify exactly what category a particular martial art falls into. Just like anything else, when first exploring the world of martial arts the perspective student should first educate themselves before determining what art is right for them.

The martial arts can be broken up into 4 broad categories. They are Education only, Spiritual, Sport, and Combative. Each of these categories will be defined.

The Educational arts are ones that, for the most part, have no real world application. These arts are usually hundreds if not thousands of years old. These martial arts generally included training in ancient weapons such as long bow, sword, shield, chain weapons, and others. Most people train in these martial arts just for the sake of the training and the enjoyment that's derived from learning about ancient methods of combat. Kenjutsu is an example of just such an art.

Spiritual martial arts encourage the development of the spirit through practicing the physical movements of the art. Many of these martial arts had their roots in combat but over the centuries have evolved to the point where the spiritual quest is what's important more than the ability to fight or wage war. Shao Lin is an example. The Shao Lin monks dedicate themselves to a life of servitude and work their entire lives to perfect reach enlightenment through their martial art.

Sport martial arts are generally not as old as the others. Many sport forms are only about 100 years old whereas the arts already mentioned above are at least a thousand years old. The focus of these martial arts is to learn to use combative principles and movements and make them appropriate for a situation where two combatants are trying to beat each other but not hurt, injure, or kill each other. These martial arts are the most prevalent in todays culture and are a lot of fun. Students have the opportunity to compete and test their skills while challenging themselves in a safe and regulated manner. Examples include Tae Kwon Do, Boxing, Wrestling, Gracie Jiu-Jitsu, Kick Boxing and MMA (mixed martial arts).

The last category has fewer students and martial art dojos then the others. The combative martial arts is a very small category. In these martial arts students learn to defend themselves in real world situations. These martial arts teach students to use sometimes lethal methods to protect themselves and often teach both ancient and modern weapons. These martial arts aren't for everyone. Many students have difficulty accepting the mind-set and view point that these arts take. These martial arts however are the ones usually adopted by police and military to train their combatants. Examples of this martial art include Ninjutsu, Jujutsu, and Sessen Jutsu.

What separates the different categories is generally mind set and the intent of training. Frequently the different arts from across the categories look the same when performed. Many techniques appear the same to the new student. What differentiates them is the intent of the training. If, for example, the martial artist is practicing with an ancient weapon that has no practical application in todays world then it certainly isn't a combative martial art. If students are learning methods of fighting that involve defending themselves against modern day weapons and methods of attack then it likely is a combative martial art.

The first thing all people who are new to the martial arts should do is educate themselves as to the different types of martial arts and the different types of training that are available.

How to pick the right Martial Arts Club
Feb 2009
Gateway Gazette

Once you've decided on beginning training in martial arts the next step is to select a club that's going to be a good fit for you. Remember that martial arts training should be an enjoyable experience and you should look forwards to every class. Below are some tips to help you find a club that's right for you.

Know what category of martial art you're interested in.

As discussed in previous articles there are 5 basic categories. They are sport, combat, educational, fitness, and ????. Before selecting a martial arts club you need to have in mind what type of training you're looking for. If you want to be in competitions for example then a combat orientated martial art isn't for you. Likewise if you want to learn effective street survival techniques then a sport art isn't a right fit. Make sure you take some time to educate yourself and understand these different categories before
beginning your search.

Know what type of martial art you're looking for. After answering what category now you have to begin asking yourself what martial art specifically. For example Gracie Barra Jiu-Jitsu and Tae Kwon Do are both sport martial arts but are very different from each other. Do you want a martial art that teaches mainly striking, kicking, punching, grappling, ground fighting, etcetera. With educational and combat martial arts are you interested in learning about traditional weapons, modern weapons, empty hand only, are you interested in a rank structure involving tests and belt levels? Once you have a specific martial art in mind do your homework to learn as much as you can about it before searching for a club that offers that training.

Know what the rates are in your area.

Now that you know what type of training and in what martial art you want to seek out learn what it costs in your area. Contact as many different clubs that offer that martial art to learn what reasonable rates are.

Phone the clubs.

Now that you've collected all your research and you know what training you want and what you're willing to spend start calling the clubs in your area. Ask the instructors what type of training they offer, what their schedule is, and how much classes cost. If everything sounds good ask to come and participate in a class. If the instructor tells you that you can't participate then request that you at least come watch a class. Internet search the club and instructor. Before attending a class spend some time online and see what you can learn. Most clubs have a website. Enter some martial arts chat forums and see what people say about the club, the instructors, and art itself. Take everything with a grain of salt but be armed with knowledge before attending a class.

Attend a class.

If a martial arts instructor won't let you at least watch a class be very leery about that club. Before making a monetary commitment to club make sure you can participate in at least one class. Watch the instructor for technical knowledge and teaching ability. Some people are very good at martial arts but that doesn't mean they're good teachers. Ask to see the instructor(s) references and credentials. Ask the other students what they like and dislike about class. Watch the instructor for negative attitude. Do they treat all students fairly? How long have they been teaching? How long has the club been around? How many students attend? Have there ever been any injuries? Are they first aid trained? Is there a first aid kit on hand? These are the types of questions you need to ask when interviewing instructors and clubs.

In conclusion make sure you're armed with knowledge before making any commitments. If you get a bad feeling about the club or an instructor it likely isn't the place for you. Good instructors want to see all their students improve and prosper and enjoy training. A good instructor will put his students well fare above all else and will train with passion and enthusiasm. Look for these important qualities when selecting martial arts training and you can enjoy a life time of challenging and rewarding experience.

Dare to Soar
February 2009
Monthly Student Newsletter

In January Marilyn, Katie, and I attended the Dare to Soar conference hosted by Winning Mind Training. All the speakers who presented were amazing and opened their hearts to share their stories with the audience. It was an incredible experience and I'm certain that everyone in attendance took with them tools that will enrich their lives. For those of you who were unable to attend I'd like to take this opportunity to share some of those lessons with you.

The most profound message for me was to expect success out of every situation. Too often I find myself dwelling on all the things I think could go wrong in a situation before I'm even involved in it. More often then not, however, none of those bad things happen. What a waste of energy all the worrying was! By expecting success in everything we do and are involved in we focus our energies on the positives and expect ourselves to perform in the most desirable way, instead of setting ourselves up for a negative experience.

For me the second most powerful message from the day was to help others to soar with me. For the last few years my life has been a quest for self-improvement. One of the most important steps along that quest was opening the FTS Training Center in Okotoks. As a teacher I now find myself in a spot where I can challenge others to take their heads out of the sand and spread their wings to soar. Once we begin making positive life changes we can share that powerful gift with others in our lives.

The third lesson I'd like to share from the seminar is that self-fulfillment isn't just your right as a human being; it's your duty. It's your job to realize your maximum potential. Not to fear success but to strive for it, to continuously work to realize your maximum potential and to challenge yourself everyday to reach it.

The fourth and last lesson I'll share with is to ask yourself this question, "What's Important Now." The host of the seminar, Brian Willis, presents this as the most important question in life. By continuously asking ourselves What's Important Now, we stay focused on what's important in our lives and what we need to be doing at that precise moment to be successful. Since following this philosophy I've found myself wasting less time and being able to stay focused on what I know I should be doing.

Training with intent
March 2009
Monthly Student Newsletter

When training in combatives it's important to not only train the body, but to train the mind also. Often if refer to the subconscious mind as a Rolodex. When we come across a situation the mind flips through the Rolodex for the solution to the problem. It looks for memories of similar situations and applies what worked in that situation to the new situation. This is one reason why I insist students in my combatives programs experience force-on-force training. It creates a memory of a situation and writes a card into the Rolodex.

Because the subconscious mind is our emotional center it remembers best situations in which emotion was attached. Highly trained professional warriors often refer to "putting on the face" when they engage in training. What they're referring to is entering an emotional state of readiness and "intent" which mirrors what they feel in a real situation.

What does this mean for us? It means that just showing up for training isn't enough. When you're there you have to engage your emotions in the training. You have to "put on the face" and train with intent. How do you do that? The simplest way is to stop telling yourself that you're in the Dojo. Start imagining that every time you're engaged in training that it's a real life situation and your safety depends on you taking measures to keep yourself alive and whole. Engage your imagination and use your mind as much in your training as your body.

The second tool is imagery drill. When you're not training with a partner close your eyes and imagine a situation where you're being attacked. Then imagine applying the skills you've learned in class to the situation at hand and imagine a successful result.

Remember that your subconscious mind doesn't know the difference between reality and fantasy. Just by using the two tools I've listed above you can engage your mind in your training and get an emotional attachment to the physical skills you're learning. Once you do this in your training will begin to become more real to your mind. You'll retain what you've learned better and longer and learn new skills faster. What's more important is it'll write that file into your Rolodex in case you ever need it in real life.

Walking the path
April 2009
Monthly Student Newsletter

What's meant by the term "warrior?" If we look at Webster's online dictionary one definition is "a man engaged or experienced in warfare." But there's much more to being a warrior than just being engaged in, or experienced in, warfare.

For feudal Japanese culture the rank and class structure were very important. Near the top of this class structure were the Samurai. Even within the Samurai class though there was a rank structure and throughout history there were those who stood out. To be more than just a soldier, to be regarded as a warrior, a person had to live there life a certain way, by a certain code of conduct.

In ancient Europe the same was true. Knights and Paladins were held in higher regard than other soldiers. They were expected to live by a certain code of conduct. When one of the members of this group didn't live up to those expectations he was frowned upon by the people.

So what makes warriors special? What is this code of conduct? Below I've provided some examples of what I think a warrior should do to be seen as a warrior.

Strive to do what is right. This often means taking the darker, more challenging, less travelled path. Remember this, when you don't know what to do, do what is right.
Continually challenge the world around you. A warrior doesn't except things at face value. Just because something's been done a certain way for a long time doesn't mean its right. Challenge the status quo and urge others to grow by doing so.
Strive to improve your understanding of the world. Seek out knowledge of all types, not just martial knowledge. Engage in a variety of activities and interests and work to be the best in every one of them. In the past warriors were often also artists, scientists, poets, song writers, actors, and authors.

Remain competitive. Don't be content with just being good enough to pass. Challenge yourself everyday to be the best at your profession and interests. Continually strive to beat old records and plateaus.

Bring others with you. One of the biggest challenges of a warrior is to recognize that spark in someone else and encourage it to grow and flourish. Don't hoard your knowledge but rather share it openly with the world. Only in this way do we all grow and pass establish our legacy with future generations.

A Matter of Science
May 2009
Gateway Gazette

If you read the first line on the FTS website (located at www.foothillstrainingservices.com) it reads, "Foothills Training Services (FTS) is committed to the instruction of quality esoteric and contemporary fighting sciences..." I wrote that sentence over two years ago to illustrate the importance of science in Martial Arts.

No other "artist" has to master such an understanding of science as a Martial Artist. The musician doesn't have to understand how sound vibrations are interpreted by the eardrum, the Chef doesn't have to understand how food particles are interpreted by the tongue, and the painter doesn't have to understand how the spectrum of light relays information to the nerves in our eyes, in order for them to be masters in their arts.

The Martial Artist however needs to have an almost post-secondary degree understanding of physics, biology, and kinesiology to become a master in their art. When a a true master of combat moves he uses soft tissue damage, skeletal damage, pain compliance, or skeletal manipulation to overcome their opponent. I often refer to this blend of physics, biology, and kinesiology as "bio-physics." The Martial Artist however needs to also be a historian, a student of language and often writing, and must understand the physics of weapons as well.

This idea isn't new. I have recently learned from my Sensei that the Japanese had a term "koppo" for describing the skeletal structure. Koppo-Jutsu is the true technique of understanding the skeletal structure. Not just the opponent's, but ours as well. This word has been in the Japanese language for at least 1000 years, if not longer.

However, it's not entirely accurate to call a master of combat a scientist. Although it is true that an actual master is constantly researching, observing, theorizing, and testing, there's more to it than just that. I true master moves with agility and finesse that can only be described as artistic. They apply the science they've learned into combat in a way that can't be described as science, but is rather an art that is a blend of all the lessons that their science has taught them.

    This is our goal as Martial Artists. To blend the various sciences of our craft together into a beautiful, although deadly, work of art.

Training for Chaos
June 2009
Monthly Student Newsletter

Lately I've begun training in a much more chaotic fashion. I used to create lesson plans and follow set programs and training methods. However I realized that human interpersonal conflict does not follow a pattern or method or make any sense. As a matter of fact it's the exact opposite. It's a chaotic creature that is constantly changing.

Even beyond training for an actual incident though, Ninjutsu is supposed to enhance every aspect of our lives. The lessons learned through training combatives can most often times be applied to other areas of our lives. The tactics and principles should enrich every aspect of our lives.

I've realized that control over our lives is an illusion. Everything we can think we're in control of can change in the span of a heartbeat. Life can be taken or created. With once word from someone else the universe as we know can come crumbling down. With the stroke of a pen or press of a keyboard letter the direction of our lives can be drastically altered.

Even our own actions aren't fully under our control. Reflexes and sympathetic responses can't be controlled. Our emotions can completely overwhelm us and cause us to act out of character.

So why then train in a "system", or method of training that relies on routine, planned responses, and doesn't take into account the constant changing universe around us. Everything we can see, touch, smell, taste, and even imagine, from the microscopic to the cosmic is in a constant state of change and flux. Thinking that we control our world is an illusion.

Instead accept that you don't have control over your world. You are a part of an ever changing, ever growing, and ever moving universe. Change, grow, and move with it. Learn to be comfortable with chaos by practicing spontaneity whenever possible. Avoid over planning. Revel in confusion and the unknown.

In these ways you can begin to learn to adapt to chaotic, violent, unknown events as they unfold around you and you will begin training yourself to persevere in the face of danger.

We All Need Teachers
July 2009
Monthly Student Newsletter

Sometimes in a warriors lifetime we can fall into the trap of closing our minds to learning. Whether we be professional warriors or martial artists we can fall into the trap of complacency and think that we've learned all there is to know or that because we're the teacher we have nothing left to learn.

One of the best ways to get out of the pitfall of complacency is to attend a class. Be a student again. Even if only for a day or two. Open your mind to learning from someone else and see the world from their point of view. Realize that there's always more knowledge to be had and that you'll never learn it all.

Bruce Lee shared this idea with his students in a cup analogy. His concept is that your mind is like a cup. When it becomes full you can't learn any more, you can't more anymore knowledge in. However we can "empty" our cup to create room for new knowledge and experiences.

If you do attend a seminar or class try to look at it from a new students point of view. Too often we can get wrapped up in criticizing the teacher. Their techniques, ability to teach, knowledge of the subject. Try to just enjoy the experience.

Often in martial arts as instructors we say that the best place to be is as a white belt. There are no expectations of a white belt, no responsibilities, and the whole world of the art in discussion is new and wonderful and magic. Whenever you attend a class as a student try to see it from a white belts point of view, regardless of your expertise in the subject. Just enjoy the class and remember what it's like to just be a student.

Remember too that this experience is just limited to specific areas. If you're a cop try taking an outdoors class, a fitness class, or how about a dance class. If you're a martial artist challenge yourself with a pottery class, or how about poetry?

By attending classes it can relight your passion for learning and challenge your knowledge, views, and opinions. Remember from time to time empty your cup and be the white belt.

What kind of Warrior are you?
August 2009
Monthly Student Newsletter

Recently while going through some personal turmoil my Sensei and I had a really cool conversation where I began to realize what kind of warrior I am. Let me illustrate with my own experience.

In martial arts we often look to 5 elements to describe personalities and characteristics of people, objects, and techniques. The elements are Earth, Fire, Water, Wind, Wood, and Void. Each has their own unique characteristics. Earth is very hard and resilient and heavy. Fire is very energetic, moving, consuming, and destroying. Water is very viscous and adapts to situations by moving and bending around them. Wind is very elusive and seems to do work without ever really tangible. Wood has energy of growth and life. And void is very mystical, almost omnipotent and exists in the past, present, and future all at the same time.

Each of us has characteristics of each element. You can see it come out in the way a martial artist moves and fights. You can also see it in a person's personality. Stubbornness is a earth characteristic, temper to fire, cool headedness to water, emotionally caring to wind, ever growing and learning to wood, and wisdom to void. This is a very simplistic explanation and my own opinion but I'm sure you get the idea and could create a list of people you know that fall under each category.

So back to my recent experience. I was having some tough times and had done three things to calm my mind and focus. The first thing was while camping I sat near a set of violent rapids in a river and just stared off into the water and enjoyed the sound and let the water babble to me. The second was some gardening. I was planting and weeding my flowerbed and attempting to coax the dirt to support my plants. And the third and most profound was to sit staring into a camp fire for endless hours and just let the flames consume my thoughts, worry, and doubt.

    While conversing with my Sensei I mentioned these 3 things and he replied that it speaks to what kind of warrior I am. As I gave it more thought it began to make sense to me. My favorite techniques are fire techniques. Violent, explosive, consuming, destructive ones. I often get hot under the collar when dealing with situations and used to have a real problem with my temper. Earth and water techniques are tied for me. I like the feel of rooting myself to smash an opponent but also really enjoy flowing around an attack and exploiting weaknesses and cracks in my opponent and flowing through movement. I also love being in the water and working with the earth.

    A further realization came to me. One that I had told my students before but really makes sense now. Each one of us has to move and react and live our own way. I'm naturally very fire orientated. Instead of being ashamed or shying away or trying to change it each of us should embrace the elements inside of us and celebrate our personality as our strength, so long as we remember to be mindful of the others too.

The MMA Explosion
August 2009
Gateway Gazette

In 1993 the first UFC hit the world. This event was created by the Gracie family to showcase their martial arts style. A martial arts event of this magnitude had never been attempted before. The first fight staged for this martial arts revolution. In it Tae Kwon Do fighter Gerard Gordeau kicked the teeth out of Sumo fighter Taila Tuli. This extreme display of martial skill shocked viewers and competitors alike and set the stage for a martial arts revolution.

For the first few UFC's the matches were fighters from different fighting styles testing their styles against each other. There were no weight classes or protective equipment and very few rules. For a period of time through the late '90's and early new millennium the UFC changed its format to include round times, weight classes, protective equipment, and safety rules. However this new format was not a hit with the fans and viewership decreased dramatically. Once Dana White took over the UFC he breathed new life into it. Thanks to aggressive new marketing and advertising the UFC is once again revolutionizing the martial arts world.

Young people from around the world are discovering the UFC and Mixed Martial Arts. Thanks to this exciting martial arts phenomenon people around the globe are getting excited about training in martial arts and discovering everything that training can offer.

So what exactly is MMA? MMA stands for Mixed Martial Arts. The term comes from the original concept where multiple martial arts styles were mixed in competition. Now however mixed martial arts means more of a style that is composed by mixing the training of several other arts. To be competitive in MMA a fighter needs to know striking, grappling, wrestling, and submission skills. For this reason the techniques and principles of Ju-Jutsu, Gracie Barra Jiu-Jitsu, Boxing,

Wrestling, and Thai Kick Boxing, are "mixed" into one training regime to lead to an all around skilled competitor. Students in MMA are exposed to techniques from these different martial arts as well as sportsmanship, competitive spirit, and discover a lot about themselves through the rigors of training.

The MMA student must remember however that training in MMA isn't the same as training in traditional martial arts and that MMA is a sport martial art and not a combative martial art and that the techniques learned are not as desirable for self defense or preservation as in a combative martial art.

The Benefits of Martial Arts Training
September 2009
Gateway Gazette

There are several benefits of training in martial arts, whether they are sport, educational, or combative arts.

Benefit #1: Fitness

In today's world our lifestyle has become more lethargic. Drive through and fast food, drive through banks, convenience meals, and a busy work schedule has led to a lifestyle where health and wellness isn't paramount in people's minds. Regardless of what kind of martial arts you train in there is an anaerobic and an aerobic component, as well as a flexibility component, to the training. Getting out to regular classes and moving your body is healthy and can help you live longer, healthier, and happier.

Benefit #2: Stress Reduction

The combination of physical exercise and movement combined with the focus and autogenic training can all help relieve stress. Some physicians estimate that up to 90% of disease is stress related. Training in martial arts is great tool for alleviating and reducing the distress of daily life.

Benefit #3: Sense of Team Work

Even though martial art training is an individual activity it is performed in a group atmosphere. The bonds and friendships formed in the dojo can last for life. I met one of my best friends through martial arts classes. This sense of belonging to a dojo and a tradition with ceremonies and history can be a fantastic feeling of teamwork for people who aren't interested in team sports.

Benefit #4: Sense of Accomplishment

When beginning the martial arts as a new student it can be very intimidating. As you train and reach new benchmarks you can reflect on what you've accomplished and how far you've come. Within a relatively short period of time you can be performing physical acts and feats that you never imagined you could. Awards, trophies, belts, and certificates can all give a sense of pride and accomplishment.

Benefit #5: Focus and Discipline

As discussed at length in previous articles, the focus and discipline learned through martial arts training will translate into other parts of your life.

Benefit #6: Self Confidence

When training in combative martial art and when you learn to effectively protect yourself and your loved ones the veil of fear and anxiety is often times lifted. Students feel more secure and confident. Don't let sport and educational martial arts give you a false sense of security though, and remember that even the most seasoned student can be hurt in a fight.

These are just some of the benefits of martial arts training. The path of a martial arts students, often referred to as *budo*, or *bushido*, translates over into their entire lives. I hear many times from my students how martial art training has enriched their lives and created more opportunity in their lives. If you have never trained in martial arts but think that it sounds appealing to you research what your area has to offer you. Good luck and happy training!

Discipline in the martial arts.
September 2009
Monthly Student Newsletter

Often people ask what are the benefits of martial arts training and is one discipline better than another. There are certain benefits that are gained by training in any martial art. They are physical fitness, flexibility, physical endurance, increased confidence, and discipline, or shugyo.

I've recently been re-introduced to this idea of Shugyo by my sensei who presented it to me in a new light that shed a new perspective on it for me. In our busy lives we are caught up in moving on to the next thing. Living the next experience. Rush to the next destination. Our society is very goal orientated and not journey orientated. Rarely are we encouraged to take time to "smell the roses" or enjoy the journey and where we're at in the moment.

The idea of Shugyo is being disciplined to your art. Some martial artists spend their lives learning many different systems of fighting but never really master any one. They don't take the time to peel back all the layers of one system and explore all it has to offer. Instead they reach a level of competence and move on to the next. They rush through their classes watching the clock anticipating the drive home, or preparing meals for the next day, or watching their favorite TV show after class. They're not living in the moment.

Martial arts can help you to develop this discipline to take the time to master something. As another colleague puts it "the pursuit of excellence." Training helps us to slow down and master our foundation before we move on to higher-level skills. It helps us to learn to live in the moment and not worry about the past or future but to be in the present and focus on our task. Training helps us to develop Shugyo.

It doesn't matter what martial art you study. Take the time to develop mastery and excellence in it. Slow down and enjoy the journey. Don't worry about your next level or test. Enjoy building your foundations and pursuing excellence. Develop the discipline to set the rest of the world aside for your training time and live in the present.

Self Protection for the Common Man
December 2009
Monthly Student Newsletter

Recently I watched the ninjutsu documentary called "Shinobi: Winds of the 34 Generations." For those of you who haven't seen it I highly recommend it. Throughout the movie several important figures in Bujinkan Ninjutsu are interviewed, including Robert Bussey. During his interview near the end of the movie he comments that self defense should be for the common man, not just the talented.

When I heard Robert Bussey say that it really got me thinking about my journey in ninjutsu. I would defiantly categorize myself as a "common man." Never in my life have I been extraordinary at anything. In fact everything I've ever been good at took a lot of work for me to be good at it and if I didn't maintain my skill it would deteriorate quite quickly. Ninjutsu and teaching are no exception. Both skills took a lot of work for me to develop and require my time and dedication to maintain and build those skills.

So what does this mean for you? It means that regardless of where you are in the journey of your life it's not too late to start training in martial arts. Training in martial arts can teach you life saving skills that you may someday need to protect yourself or your loved ones or beliefs.

You don't need to be talented or gifted. You don't need to be an athlete. Self protection is for the everyday person. And as you develop skills and its amazing how much your self confidence will grow. Martial arts are about more of a self discovery than it ever is about learning to hurt other people. Every martial artists goal is to develop themselves and protect themselves, not about hurting other people.

So regardless of where you are on your path of life I encourage each of you to get out and train. Maybe you've been away for awhile, perhaps you've never trained. Maybe you don't think you have the time or ability. You don't need to have a lot of time, as little as 20 minutes a day is better than nothing, you don't need to be fit or athletic or skilled, training will give you all those things, that's why we do it. Don't be intimidated if you've never trained before, we all start somewhere.

I hope I've lit a fire in each of you to begin training, get back to training, or to continue to train with zeal and passion. I hope 2009 was good to each of you. Thanks for all your support. Merry Christmas and well wishes for 2010!

Listening to your instincts.
February 2010
Monthly Student Newsletter

Recently I was the victim of a fraud scam. Although I use the word "victim" that isn't quite right. It's my own fault for not listening to my instincts. It was an expensive lesson to learn.

Gavin DeBecker explains in his book "The Gift of Fear" why listening to your fear is a positive survival mechanism. When we have fear it's because a part of us has experienced or observed something out of the ordinary in our environment. I know some of you subscribe to a different philosophy that we actually feel other people's intent with our spirit. For the purpose of this discussion it doesn't matter what philosophy you prescribe to, the mind model theory or the intent belief. All that matters is that we can perceive when "something's not right" with what's happening around us.

DeBecker goes on to explain that when people are victims of crime they can often look back over the event(s) and pick out when they thought something wasn't right and can remember choosing to ignore that "gut instinct."

This is exactly what happened to me. While selling some items over the internet I was contacted by a potential customer. We communicated for several weeks and arranged a mutually agreeable deal for some gym mats I had for sale. Then the buyer started making strange requests for me to accept a large some of money for them, keep my money for the mats, and forward the rest to the shipper. This was reminiscent of a scam I had arrested someone for years previous. What changed however was that I requested the funds in a certain format and the other party agreed.

At this point I ignored what my instinct was telling me and talked myself into trusting the other party. Every warrior inch of me told me that it was a mistake but I convinced myself it would be ok and that surely I couldn't be taken advantage of. I even talked it over with some warrior brothers who agreed it was a scam, but then I convinced them that it would be ok and there wasn't anything nefarious going on.

A week later after my bank accounts were frozen and I was out $1200. Although the loss sucks it reminded me of how important it is to listen to my instincts. Whether or not I recognized the scam on a subconscious level or felt the other parties intent doesn't really matter for the sake of this discussion. What does matter is that as warriors we develop combat instincts. We learn to read situations and people. When you get that gut feeling that something isn't right, listen to it!!! Learn to listen to and trust those instincts and feelings and please learn from my mistake and don't ignore them.

What is Ninpo???
March 2010
Gateway Gazette

Ninpo is a word that is closely associated with Ninja and Ninjutsu. Remember that Nin 忍 is made with two characters Edge of the Blade (Ha) over Heart (Shin). Nin means perseverance, patience, or stealth depending on how it's used. This is a very powerful character though and as one makes their way through life learns that "perseverance" means many different things. The character Po 法 means Philosophy. Ninpo therefore can be translated as "The philosophy of perseverance."

This may seem straight forward but, as is the case with a lot of Japanese translation, it's more difficult then that. First of all, what is the philosophy of perseverance? What is the philosophy of stealth? Or patience? What does that mean? As a student of Budo and Bujutsu I was often told that Ninpo was religious, that it was a type of Shinto based around the Ninja coming to terms with living their life the way they had to and how they accepted doing the things they had to ensure their survival and that of their families.

Bud Malstrom in Shinobi Winds tells us that Ninpo isn't religious, that it's a way of life but doesn't have any religious meaning, that it can be shared with and experienced by people of all religions. Hatsumi Sensei says that Ninpo is "wisdom for life." But what does any of that mean.

I've been practicing martial arts in some way shape or form since being introduced to boxing by my step dad 22 years ago. I've been studying martial arts seriously for the last 14 years and Bujinkan Ninjutsu for 13 of those years and have been making a living teaching martial and warrior arts for the last 5 years. I'm not telling you this to pad my own ego. Rather to relay to you that after all this time I think I finally have an understanding what Ninpo is all about.

It boils down to mindset. Ninpo is a state of mind. It's a way of thinking and applying yourself and seeing the world. It's a state of preparedness. Brian Willis talks a lot about the "Winning Mind" and others teach us about "Bulletproof Mind" or the "Survivors Mindset" or the "Warrior Spirit." These are all examples of Ninpo.

Ninpo for me is that state of readiness always. Other martial artists teach warrior arts and combat methods, both armed and unarmed. But I see a lot of them miss this element of readiness. They train for certain encounters and most of them I have a lot of respect for what they're doing. But they never apply it. What good is learning how to defend yourself if you never look at a real world application? If you don't switch on and prepare yourself? Ninpo is that preparation.

Lets look at some examples. When driving your car do you lock the doors (that is if they don't have an auto lock feature)? Do you avoid situations that you know increase the likelihood of being attacked? When flying do you request an aisle seat so that you can react in case of a hijacking or do you request a window seat so you can sleep for the entire flight? When you're training are you imagining a real life attack or simply going through the motions? When preparing to fly do you plan on taking a steel pen and/or wooden cane so that you're armed in case of an encounter? Do you where long sleeve shirts so that you can use magazines and newspapers as makeshift armour? When you walk into a restaurant do you sit with your back to a wall near a window so that you can escape in case of a fire and can't be ambushed? When you're standing alone in a bus shelter are you aware of who's coming in and out and are you prepared with "when-then" thinking?

These are all examples of Ninpo. The philosophy of perseverance is about preparedness. The boy scouts motto is "be prepared." That is what Ninpo is all about.

What is Budo???
April 2010
Monthly Student Newsletter

Budo is often a term thrown quite often in martial arts. Generally speaking senior students and instructors understand the term. "Budo" translates from Japanese to English as "Warrior Way." Often the term "Bushido" is also used.

As so often with Japanese martial arts concepts though the translation doesn't explain what the term means. If you ask 100 different martial artists you'd probably get 100 different responses. Everything from "I don't know" to who knows how many explanations.

I'd like to take a moment to share my explanation. I think "Budo" is the constant refinement of ones self. A constant looking inward, assessing, planning, and action to improve yourself. It is a constant polishing of the mind, body, and spirit. A never ending process of assessing your limitations and barriers and working to break through them.

In this way the warrior becomes like a sword. A sword left in its scabbard laying in a corner somewhere uncared for begins to tarnish, then rust, then becomes useless. Compared to the sword that is cared for, maintained, constantly inspected for flaws, sharpened, worked, and polished. This sword becomes a work of art. A thing to be admired and respected. A truly useful tool to save lives.

The martial artist is exactly the same. If you don't train, don't do your research, work hard, sweat in the dojo, or even go to the dojo, you're like the first sword. If, however, you train regularly, practice the martial arts, train hard and with purpose and intent, then you become the weapon to save lives, an artist that will be admired, and respected by their peers and others.

If you're the first sword, fear not!!! That old rusty sword lying in the corner covered in a layer of dust, it's got one very powerful thing going for it. It's got unlimited possibility. With some care, effort, and work, it can become the polished weapon that everyone "oooo's" and "awwwe's" about.

Just like the person who's never trained before, or perhaps has been away from training for some time. Apply a little bit of work, and you'll be amazed at the things you can accomplish.

For me this process is "Budo." A constant inspection of myself and sharpening and polishing in the quest for perfection.

Challenging Yourself
May 2010
Monthly Student Newsletter

Recently I was attending a training conference in the US for law enforcement trainers. The conference is a blend of instructor development, certification, and social networking. This was my 4th time in attendance and I was taking 2 instructors level certification classes. For the last several years I've spent more time as an instructor then as a student and have found I have certain Uke's that I prefer to demo on because I know how they move and react and their Ukemi during a demo.

In my first instructor level class there was about 20 of us training. The material was rather basic for me and I found I was getting a little bored of the material. Then I made the decision to not think as an instructor who's been involved in martial arts and survival tactics for 22 years, but rather as a student with an opportunity to work on my skills without the restraints of instructing.

There was a really, and I mean really, big guy on the course. He must've been over 6.5 feet tall and I bet just shy of 300lbs. He was in good shape and was really intimidating. As soon as our instructor told us to find a partner of our choice I made the decision to find him and train with him.

I could've taken it easy for the whole course but instead I decided to challenge myself mentally and physically. I wanted to put myself to the test. I've been telling students for years that size doesn't matter and forcing them into situations where they need to work with someone bigger and stronger then them. It was time for Sensei to put his money where his mouth is.

It was refreshing when I was able to control this guy who's about twice my size using simple Tai Jutsu and the technique the instructor had requested we work on. I truly felt as though all my years on the mats were validated and that I can truly say to my students that size doesn't matter. I had worked with bigger guys before but nothing like this!

So the next time you're training and you know that you have your favorite partners to work with because you connect with each other, challenge yourself to work with someone different. When you're successful your confidence in what you're training will sky rocket and you'll be better prepared for an altercation.

Myths of Self Defense
June 2010
Monthly Student Newsletter

Myth #1: It'll never happen to me

There is a difference between paranoia and preparedness, but living in denial of danger is flat out reckless. We live in a world where people are victims of violent crime for an entire spectrum of reasons, all the way from someone else robbing the victim to acquire resources for their own survival to offenders attacking and murdering innocents for perverse joy. The chance of being a victim of a violent crime in Canada is low, but there is still a chance. Living by the ostrich technique, that is sticking your head in the sand thinking that because you don't see danger there's none out there, is not sufficient to protect yourself. Be aware of dangers and trends in your community and take steps to be prepared and to prepare your family and loved ones. An ounce of preparation can save lives.

Myth #2: If it does happen to me I'll be able to handle myself

During an attack you will not magically know how to protect yourself unless you've trained and prepared for self protection. Due to chemical changes in your body and brain chemistry during times of survival stress you will have difficulty thinking and problem solving. Unless you've trained gross motor skill protection techniques and mentally prepared for an attack you will not be able to adequately defend yourself. You will feel exhausted within seconds, weak and unable to fight off an attacker you will be seriously hurt or even killed. Stress inoculation training from a professional instructor is required to learn real and effective self protection skills.

Myth #3: Someone will come to my aid

There are literally hundreds, if not thousands, of documented cases where people have witnessed a violent crime and not helped the victim. There are a few reasons for this, all the way from people being frozen by fear and confusion, to people just not wanting to risk getting involved. Recently in New York City there was a case where a man who was stabbed lay bleeding to death in the doorway of an apartment building. Several people stepped over him on their way to work in the morning. One man even lifted him up an observed the wound to his torso, and set him back on his front and left. No one even called an ambulance or police as the man laid there and eventually died. During a violent attack the only person that's going to help you is you, so you had better be ready.

Myth #4: Taking a self defense class will be enough

Taking one self defense class is not enough to learn effective self protection. Knowledge is power, the more you drill gross motor skills and mentally prepare for an attack the better prepared you'll be. Understanding why people attack each other, what motivates them, how to detect attacks, and how to protect yourself without ever relying on physical techniques is the ultimate goal. Seek out an instructor who understands this and can give you the information you need to protect yourself.

Remember that learning effective Self Protection is a combination of physical, mental, and emotional training. Self Protection is all about being aware of the dangers around you and how to take simple non-invasive steps to protect yourself and the people around you. Our culture is becoming increasingly dangerous. Violent crimes include robbery, sexual assault, assault, random acts of violence, targeted violence, cross fire situations, and murder, just to name a few. Self Protection is not paranoia, it is preparedness, and is possible without making major changes to your lifestyle or regular routines. Seek out professional instruction today before you're a crime statistic.

Brotherhood
August 2010
Monthly Student Newsletter

Often in martial arts and combatives the term "brotherhood" is used. We refer to each other as "budo brother" or the "brother and sisterhood of the shield." It's been my observation though that while we use this terminology it's quite often the case where we don't treat each other with that level of respect. I've witnesses numerous martial artists and modern warriors stab each other in the back, lie about each other, cheat each other, and steal from each other. Even if not to this extreme many warriors today do not show each other the respect that a "brother" or "sister" deserves. Instead they act in a disrespectful manner and as a group we tolerate it.

How did this happen? Where did it come from? Who started it? Better yet, who cares? The fact of the matter is if you're going to use that language then be brave enough to back it up with action. Words without action are shallow and meaningless. They are empty. They have no meaning. Words backed by action however can be a powerful catalyst for change. One person being brave enough to treat others with respect and to help each other imagine what we can accomplish. One warrior on their own can inspire a lot of change and good in the world, so imagine for a moment what an entire team, or even better and entire generation, of warriors working together could accomplish.

Some of you may run your own business. You may be thinking, "But if I do that I could lose my students." True, you might. As you educate your students to other possibilities they may decide that you're not the teacher for them or that they're more interested somewhere else. But you'd probably lose that student anyways. They'll probably figure that out for themselves eventually. And when they do they might become resentful of you for withholding from them. If however you were honest from the beginning, told them about other possibilities, shared knowledge with other instructors and schools and warriors, and exposed them to other ideas, those students will likely leave and still respect you and say good things about you to others. By showing respect to others and by sharing your ideas you create an environment where people want to share with you. In the long run you learn much more and surround yourself with positive like minded warriors.

For example I was at a hot yoga class a few weeks ago. The instructor was great. As I was waiting by the front door to leave another person from the class engaged the instructor in conversation. The student, as it turns out, was an instructor from another yoga studio that teaches the exact same class. They began comparing how they run their class and were genuinely excited to discuss it with each other. By the end of the conversation the "student" was inviting the "instructor" to her class. What I realized was that they both understand that in fact they themselves are students, and that to grow you need to let down those walls and have genuine conversations with each other.

I encourage you all to learn from the two yoga instructors and let down your walls. If you're going to use terms like "brother" and "sister" then back it up with action. Share your ideas openly and treat others with respect, and that same energy will be returned upon you exponentially.

Winning
September 2010
Monthly Student Newsletter

Recently I was training a group of students who seemed to be having a difficult time getting motivated. We took a break from our physical training and I asked them what the word "Winner" meant to them. We came up with an exhaustive list of buzzwords such as; champion, someone who puts in the time to train repetition after repetition of the same skill, passion, and someone who comes in first place.

One of the things I found very interesting is what the term winner meant to younger students compared to older students. Younger students for the most part thought that a winner was someone who came in first place in competition. Older students leaned more to believe that a winner was someone who had a certain personality and who conducted themselves in a certain way.

As I facilitated the conversation I began to ask myself, "what do I think a winner is?" Well, for me a winner is someone who is self motivated. Someone who pushes themselves to be the best person they can be every day. Someone who is self aware of their shortcomings and fears and who has the courage to face those and challenges themselves to overcome them. Someone who has passion for life and cares about who they are, what they do, and how they conduct themselves. A winner isn't necessarily the person who wins every contest, or comes in first all the time, but is the person who keeps coming back to the competition even when they've lost, who keeps training, who keeps pushing themselves. A winner is a leader, even if they're only leading themselves.

I made the comment to the class that I don't train losers. I refuse to train losers. I only train winners. My goal at FTS is to not only provide physical skills training for people interested in martial arts or seeking police and military training, but to also be a source of inspiration and to provide an environment where students feel empowered to be winners. To turn out people who are champions at life.

That doesn't mean that I expect my students to be the absolute best martial artists in the world. I do however expect them to be the best that they can be, to live up to 100% of their potential. To lead themselves, to motivate themselves, to push through what they think their barriers are and emerge on the other side as winners and champions.

For me this is a large part of bushido. Our individual paths as warriors. To identify our fears, apprehensions, anxieties, and the limitations we've placed on ourselves and to attack them head on and conquer them. How do we do that? A great place to start is in the dojo. I asked my students to be winners for the 90 minutes a day I have them. That when they walk through my door to put on their winner face. And if they decide to take it off when they leave then that's their choice, but when they're sharing their time with me in my space to be winners. Something tells me that after they wear their winner face for 90 minutes in the dojo, they'll want to leave it on when they leave.

Once we feel what it's like to be winner, a champion, a leader, a sheepdog, we never want that feeling to end. We never want to be losers, followers, sheep, ever again.

Giving Thanks
October 2010
Monthly Student Newsletter

Given that October is the month of Thanksgiving I thought it fitting that we all take a moment to stop and give thanks. How often do you ask yourself this question, "What am I thankful for today?" My recent observations are that for the most part, especially in North American culture, we are very wrapped up in a sense of entitlement. I think for the most part people aren't even aware that they do it. It's just a by-product of the culture we live in. Our media and our consumables all move very fast and promote a disposable culture that encourages us to always be looking to the next product, job, challenge, and sometimes even partner! No wonder it's difficult to look past a sense of entitlement and begin to develop a sense of appreciation.

So having said all that I'd like to take a moment and give thanks. First to my mom, step dad, and father. Without them I highly doubt I would have turned out the way I am today, or been given life at all for that matter! Second, to my first teachers from C.Ian Maclaren and Oilfields High school, who always were willing to take the time to help me learn and who taught me how, not what, to think. Third, I was blessed again with a great set of professors at Mount Royal University who challenged my views of the world as an adult and the role of a warrior. Since then I have had the privilege of training and serving with some of the finest warriors on the planet. I'd especially like to thank Brian Willis, Wally Muller, and Chris Butler who even though I don't get to train with or learn from on a regular basis, when I do have opportunity to attend one of their courses it defiantly takes my learning forward by leaps and bounds and encourages me to ask the question "what can I do to be better?" In the world of martial arts I am truly privileged with the honour of learning from Shihan Jay Creasey who is arguably one of the best martial artists and knowledgeable men around!

As well as the men and women above I was fortunate enough to be born in a society where learning is respected, and available. There are literally dozens of other people who's seminars I've attended, or books I've read, that I'm so thankful for the work they do and for the opportunity to have met them and learned from them.

Lastly I'd like to take an opportunity to thank my students. I have learned as much from you in the last few years as you have from me. Thanks for being hungry to learn, and for giving me the privilege to be a part of your lives.

There are many other things I'm thankful for, being born in a great country, the life I have, the lives of others that I've been fortunate enough to share for various lengths of time, for the job I have, for the fact that I have a roof over my head, shoes on my feet, clothes on my back, no one shooting at me, food to eat, and clean water to drink! Compared to some people from various parts of the world, how could I not count myself among the blessed!

And so I challenge you to sit down regularly and think to yourself, "What am I thankful for today?" This simple act of reflection can truly have a huge impact in your life, which will ripple out to touch other lives as well.

The Only Two Truths
November 2010
Monthly Student Newsletter

While teaching a group of security professionals we were discussing the idea of Adversarial Respect (see October 2010 Newsletter FTS Tactical Division Section for details) and I was having some degree of difficulty making the concept operational for them. Then it occurred to me that the whole point of Adversarial Respect is to not label people, but rather to respect the fact that they are capable of any degree of human behavior, including violence towards another human being.

I expressed the idea to the Security Officers that there really are only two things in a confrontation; the behavior you're observing, and the potential for that behavior to change. As soon as we label an adversary we limit how much respect we give them as an adversary and that could prove fatal to us. What happens when our label is incorrect? We have already committed ourselves mentally, emotionally, and physically to a course of action that we might not be able to alter in time to deal with changing circumstances.

After giving this idea some more thought and discussing it more with martial artists and health and wellness professionals I came to realize that the same idea can be applied to any aspect of the our lives. The only two things we truly have in life are what we can observe right now, and the potential for it to change.

Have you ever watched a martial artist perform a technique and somewhere along the way something goes wrong and they just stop? They have already predicted what was happening and committed themselves to a series of events. When those events don't happen of they change the martial artist freezes and doesn't know where to go or what to do next.

How about outdoors enthusiasts who begin an event predicting what the weather will be like so they don't bring extra shelter, food, water, or transportation? Police officers who judge people by what they look like or how they're dressed, slot them into a category, and find themselves injured or dead a split second later because they ignored threat cues? How about professional fighters who predict their opponent will move or operate in a certain way? What happened in the Vietnam War when the U.S. Military underestimated the fighting capability of the Viet Cong? These are all examples of situations where people thought they could predict the future and ignored or didn't see indicators of what was truly happening.

As warriors in physical altercations this idea could be life saving. But what about for everyday people? How many North Americans in the last year thought they had stable income and found themselves suddenly unemployed? How devastating mentally and emotionally was that loss?

Since thinking in this way I've become much more open to changes in the world around me. I find I'm able to better prepare for emergencies in the future.

Building a Training Program
December 2010
Monthly Student Newsletter

     Recently Soke-Dai Jeremy Braezeale of Yanagi Ryu and Elemental Combatives International visited us at FTS to host the first Call to Arms Seminar. During that time he shared some excellent knowledge and insights with us. After class times I had the privilege of long conversations where we talked about training, history, combatives, etcetera. During those conversations I began to solidify more in my own mind what I think a training regime should look like.

     A training program should be broken into stages. Each stage should be progressively more challenging than the last. Stage 1 should set the context for the skill. The history or combative context is explained. This is where I disagree with some combative instructors and agree more with Shihan Jay Creasey's methodology. The skill in its entirety at speed and resistance should be demonstrated at least once. This creates a "roadmap" in the students head of where they're going. The last thing to do in this stage is demonstrate the first "way point" of that roadmap and have the students begin working on it. This first way point should be the very first part of the skill. Generally speaking it should be performed without an opponent, depending on the skill.

     Stage 2 introduces an opponent to the student learning the skill. Targeting, range, distance, and effects of technique are learned. The opponent is merely a target at this point and offers zero resistance.

     Stage 3 begins to introduce resistance and successful application of skill to resistance. In stage 3 the opponent isn't trying to defeat the student but allowing them to experience success to resistance.

     Stage 4 introduces increased resistance and creative problem solving by the student. Flow between skills is established by using a new skill to solve failure of the previous one.

Stage 5 is often referred to as "Force-on-force" training and creates a real life scenario in which the student must use a variety of skills to achieve success. The student is also able to choose which skill they use. This stage is goal oriented and not technique oriented. The student can chose whatever skill they wish so long as that skill is tactically, morally, and legally sound. In this final stage students must deal with the threat(s) accordingly AND find extraction and escape routes AND provide first aid and self aid AND be able to communicate why they made the decisions they did.

Sage 6 occurs for athletes and professional fighters but rarely and hopefully not, for combat martial artists. Stage 6 is actually performing the skill in a combat setting.

So how many times to you perform each stage? How many reps at each stage? How many times did Michael Jordan practice a free throw in his career? Thousands? Millions? A true professional doesn't just say "ok I did this a few times and now I'm bored." Rather they seek perfection through dedicating themselves to completing hundreds of thousands of reps so when "game day" comes they move without thought.

New Year's Resolutions
December 2010
Monthly Student Newsletter

With the coming of a New Year comes an old tradition, the New Year's Resolution. The tradition was started by early Babylonians and continued by the Romans as a way to make peace with neighbors to begin the New Year without conflict and to in essence "Bury the Hatchet" from any disputes from the year before.

Many people in Western Culture make resolutions for the sake of continuing a tradition. But how many people stick with them? In my observations most people make a resolution and within a matter of days have given up on it. Some of the most popular ones are to lose weight, stop smoking, reconnect with loved ones or lost friends, travel, attend classes, get promotions, and exercise.

In fact almost every resolution I ever heard was something healthy. So why not stick with it? Most people don't stick with it because they don't have a plan. "This year I resolve to lose weight," is a great goal, but it's not a plan. To get results you must have a plan with objective measurable goals along the way.

So below are my tips for making a better you in 2011.

Start small and measurable. I.e. "I'm going to lose weight." That's a lofty goal. How about "By the end of 2011 I'm going to have lost 20lbs." "I'm going to get fit," can become "By March I'm going to be able to jog 5km without stopping." These are both smaller goals and measurable. Develop your plan. How am I going to lose the 20lbs. I need to eat healthy nutritious food. I need to stay hydrated. I need to exercise. But what if you don't know how to do any of those things? Perhaps the first step should be research your goal and get a professional to help develop the rest of the plan.

Plan stages. My new years resolution plan should be staged. I'm not going to work all year to step on the scale in 12 months for the first time. If I resolve to lose 20lbs by December 2011 I should be losing 5lbs every 3months. Instead of focusing on a 12mos goal I can focus on my mini goals every 3mos.
Surround yourself with success. Looking to lose weight? Join a club, get a trainer, work out with friends, get magazine subscriptions that educate and motivate you. Surround yourself with all the parts of a successful equation, including people who support and motivate you, not give you excuses for failure, tare you down, or otherwise limit your chances of success.

    Start with those steps and your 2011 New Years Resolution can be more than just lip service to an old tradition. It can be your equation to make a better you for 2011!!! I used the example of weight loss of this illustration but this formula can lead to success for any self improvement plan.

Why We Train
March 2011
Monthly Student Newsletter

February is a rough time of year in Canada. Christmas is over and the debt has piled up, winter is dragging on and spring's too far away to get excited about. Statistically speaking relationships fall apart and suicide increases. This is the time of year when I notice people lose interest in their training and begin to either not apply themselves with intensity in class or not attend all together.

Because of all these factors I asked myself the other day, why do I do it? Why did I leave a good paying government job to run a dojo where nothing is certain? Why for over 14 years have I been attending Bujinkan classes where I get hit, twisted, locked, thrown, and just beaten up over and over again? Why do my students do it? What makes us tick?

I asked my students to write down why they keep attending class OR what brought them to class in the first place. When I think back to why I first started attending classes the answer was simple. I was beginning school to go into law enforcement and I didn't want to get hurt on the job. Some of my students are in law enforcement also but the majority are not. I expected answers like "to learn to fight" or "to learn self protection." I was surprised at the answers.

Out of 20 students who participated in the exercise only 1 wrote anything about fighting, and that's because he's preparing for his first MMA fight. The other 19 all wrote about other values.

Some said the dojo was like a family, others said for fun and recreation. Some indicated to be active and get fit. Some people liked the historical context. Some people appreciated the educational aspect of the traditional martial arts. One student indicated that it taught her inner strength. Another indicated it prepared him to learn how not to fail.

Both my MMA and Bujinkan classes are aggressive and full contact. Students get their butts whipped regularly. All of my material is rooted in combatives, either ancient or modern. Everything we do is designed to hurt other people, either in a sport context or as self protection in lethal force encounters context. But even my students who are professional warriors didn't write about hurting other people. They wrote about improving themselves.

This is the heart of budo. The idea of shugyo. That we are improving ourselves. It's not about being better than anyone else, it's about being at the top of your own potential.

As the exercise continued I was forced to ask myself why I keep training and teaching. The answer came in the form of an epiphany. Health. Just that one word. Health. Emotional, Mental, and Physical. Exercise through training, meditation in movement, being aware of my surroundings and predicting outcomes to protect myself from accidental or intentional harm. Overall concern for my health.

For a group of students who train in a warrior art that was born out of combat and soldiering I find it amazing that none of us wrote about hurting other people, or about being better than other people. This is truly what martial arts in modern society is really about. Working on yourself. Making yourself the best that you can be and reaching your full potential as a human being.

The Importance of Cross Training
April 2011
Monthly Student Newsletter

When I first started training martial arts I fell into a very dangerous trap. I used to put down other martial arts. I thought that whatever art I was studying was superior to any others. However over the last several years I've come to realize that the different martial arts actually have more in common than they do apart. I've cross trained in 14 different martial arts. The only art I work at mastering proficiency in out of those is Bujinkan Budo Taijutsu, and some of those arts I've only trained at 1 or 2 seminars, but what I've learned from seeing all these different martial arts and trying them is that there's actually way more in common than what the average martial artist, or even most martial arts instructors, realize.

Let me illustrate with a few examples. A kimura in BJJ is the same as an oni kudaki in Bujinkan. A take jime in judo is the same as a rear naked choke in BJJ. An omote gyaku in Bujinkan is the same as a gun inversion in Hapkido. A hook punch in boxing is the same as a hooking knife stab in Balintawak Arnis. A Jeet Kune Do straight blast is the same as a katana thrust in Kenjutsu. That's not to say that these technique are done exactly the same way but in each example the core body mechanics AND the physics and anatomical principles at play are the same.

When you think about it this makes total sense. There are only so many ways to move the human body. More importantly there are only so many ways to move the human body in a way that maintains structural integrity, balance, skeletal alignment, and power. Remember also that empty hand martial arts come out of armed martial arts. Therefore it makes sense to develop a combat system that relies on the same body mechanics regardless of the weapon engaged in combat. Often if you track the lineage of a martial art back in time far enough you realize that it didn't actually originate where it's currently situated. For example Gracie Jiu Jitsu goes back to Japanese

Kodokan Judo, which goes back to Chinese Kung Fu, which goes back to Indian śastravidyā. Bujinkan Koto Ryu is another example, its lineage tracks to Cho Gyokko in China.

So what should all this mean to you? It should mean that regardless of your martial art of passion don't put down other martial arts. Each has something to offer the others. It also means that while there's nothing wrong in having pride in your particular history and lineage and striving to master one martial art, it's good to explore and be exposed to others. They may help you see your own art in a new light and help open new doors.

A few weeks ago I was attending a Bujinkan class with Shihan Jay Creasey and he had us working on spinning hook kicks. Rarely in Bujinkan do you see spinning hook kicks and he told us that the kick we were training isn't part of our system. So then why train it? It increases balance, trains the eyes to track targets in a 360 degree circle, increases flexibility in the hamstring and hip, teaches how to move and maintain relative distance and range to an opponent, and increases thigh abductor and adductor strength. Those are all things that will help with the rest of Bujinkan techniques as well as self protection and martial arts in general.

In conclusion to develop as a martial artist I would encourage you to cross train in different martial arts and keep an open mind. In the words of Soke-dai Braezeale, "there are no bad martial arts systems, just bad martial artists."

What is Bujinkan Budo Taijutsu?
May 2011
Combat Network Magazine

Over the course of the 40 years much has been said about the mystic art of Japans elite warriors, the Ninja. It can be difficult to summarize or get an understanding of what Ninjutsu is, what is learned in a Ninjutsu dojo, or how the transmissions are passed down from one generation to the next. I have been studying Ninjutsu for nearly 15 years, and most days I feel like I've barely scratched the surface. This article will provide the reader with a basic understanding of Ninjutsu and its primary organizations and teachings.

Ninjutsu is in and of itself NOT a martial art in the usual sense of the word. Ninjutsu means to study the techniques of stealth. The Kanji "Nin" 忍 in essence means "stealth" and "Jutsu" 術 means "the offensive and defensive techniques" often shortened to "the art of". Another word for this is Shinobi Iri. What most people think of as "Ninjutsu" is actually a combination of several different martial arts and skills combined into one system that incorporates both combative martial arts movements with the study of stealth and espionage. One of the reasons "Ninjutsu" is used to describe this training is because another accepted translation of "Nin" is "Perseverance". Therefore the term Ninjutsu can also be interpreted as "The Art of Perseverance". In essence this describes the Bujinkan, 1 of the 3 major systems of Ninjutsu training in existence today.

When Ninjutsu was first exposed to the it was referred to as Togakure Ryu Ninjutsu. The Togarkure Ryu is a ninja school dating back to 1161 A.D and is the oldest of the 9 Ryuha (schools) in the Bujinkan. When I started in Ninjutsu in the mid '90's nearly all school training certificates, uniform patches, and crests, labelled the school as a Togakure Ryu Ninjutsu school. Dr. Hatsumi however is also the grandmaster of 8 other martial arts schools. Only 3 out of the 9 are Ninja, or Ninpo, schools. The other 8 cover various specialty tactics and areas of armed and unarmed combat. Elements out of the 9 schools when transmitted together essentially make up Masaaki Hatsumi's school the Hatsumi Han, or Bujinkan Budo. The 9 schools of Bujutsu (Warrior Skills Training) that make up the Bujinkan are; Koto Ryu, Gyokko Ryu, Kuki Shinden Ryu, Takagi Yoshin Ryu, Shinden Fudo Ryu, Gikan Ryu, Gyokushin Ryu, Kumogakure Ryu, and Togakure Ryu. Most Bujinkan Dojo's that I've visited spend a great deal of time teaching and studying the Koto Ryu, Gyokko Ryu, Togakure Ryu, and Kukishinden Ryu.

Training in a Bujinkan Dojo should more correctly be referred to as Bujutsu rather than Ninjutsu, because several combative skills are taught simultaneously, not just stealth and espionage skills. Most Bujinkan Dojo's focus on the combative aspect of training more than the proper kata's or forms of the techniques. For this reason training in a Bujinkan Dojo can be very challenging and is one of the reasons such a small percentage of martial artists train in Bujinkan. Quit often there is very little safety gear worn or utilized. Students hit and throw each other, often bare knuckle. Because 9 martial arts systems are trained simultaneously it can be very confusing for the new student and almost overwhelming at times. Training this way affords freedom of movement however. This principle is often referred to as Tai Jutsu. Dr. Hatsumi often tells his students that this is the root of the Bujinkan system and one of the most important aspects of combat. Moving the body is essential to fighting. Because we train in 9 schools Bujinkan students learn to transition back and forth through various ranges, various weapons, various striking styles, and various grappling styles including throws, ground fighting, and standing grappling. As well strategy and espionage/stealth work is essential to the system. Combined this makes for an effective system of combat which truly encourages students to use their individual strengths to their advantage. The Bujinkan promotes freedom of movement and individuality which is expressed through your combative techniques and tactics. Some sensei refer to it as "organized chaos".

It's for these reasons that the term Bujinkan Budo Taijutsu is used instead of Ninjutsu. Bujinkan means "devine warrior house", budo is "the way of the warrior", and taijutsu is the root of our combative movement and means "offensive and defensive skills of using moving the body". Ninjutsu is only one of the skills that Bujinkan students train in.

Healers make the Best Warriors
May 2011
Combat Network Magazine

In Japan 1000 years ago there were a group of mountain ascetics called the Yamabushi. Yamabushi translates to English as "Mountain Warrior." These mountain men were more than just warriors however, they were also regarded as great healers. Throughout history many warrior classes have respected healers and even had an element of healing to their spiritual beliefs. Shaolin monks, Indian warriors, and even British Paladins all had an element of healing in their systems. Even the Spartans had a particular place in battle and in their societal hierarchy for surgeons and medics. This tradition is recognized in today's militaries, medics and healers still have a special place in the hearts and minds of warriors.

As a practitioner of Bujinkan Budo Taijutsu and a healer I gravitate towards Usui Reiki, a Japanese form of energy healing. Both these arts have elements of Yamabushi traditions. Reiki is a system of energy healing where the healer becomes a conduit for Ki, or energy. In this case Rei means Spirit or Devine. Reiki can be interpreted as Devine Energy. This is usually referred to as chigong or qigong in Chinese traditions, and Prana in Indian traditions.

Usui Reiki was developed by Mikao Usui, a Japanese Buddhist monk, in 1922 after meditation. In his system of Reiki the belief is that through meditation he gained enlightenment and learned how to channel Reiki into others to heal them. Since 1922 several forms of Japanese and Western Reiki have been developed all with similar concepts and beliefs. The primary difference between Japanese and Western Reiki is that Japanese Reiki teachings are more intuitive and encourage students and practitioners to "feel" the energy and flow, where as Western Reiki systems are much more systematic and rigid in their patterns and approach. Although Usui Reiki is often used as the base for Reiki practitioners and students the history of using Reiki to heal is reported to go back as far as 10 000 years.

The basic premise in Usui Reiki is that there are 7 chakra's through the core of each person connecting them with the heavens above and the earth below. When one of these chakras becomes blocked or negative energy attaches to it than regular Reiki energy cannot pass through the body naturally. This manifests itself in emotional, mental, and physical illness. A Reiki practitioner can focus the Reiki to these chakras to heal and open them and restore harmony and balance to the body.

There are 3 levels of practice in most Reiki systems. In level 1 a practitioner receives an Attunement which allows them to feel Reiki and use it to heal others using hand positions over a client to focus the flow of energy into trouble spots. This resembles several Christian beliefs of "Laying on Hands." In level 2 an Usui Reiki practitioner learns power symbols for clearing a space, learns how to perform distance healing, and the importance of our connection to the earth and how to use crystals to enhance the healing power of Reiki. In level 3 the practitioner becomes a Master and learns how to attune and teach others how to heal using Reiki. The term "master" in this context doesn't mean in the sense of a hierarchy but rather in respect to how to use Reiki.

Practicing Reiki has helped my martial arts in several ways. First it's taught me to be more open and receiving of feelings and energy around me. This may sound very mystic but take into account how often we hear people say, "I just had a feeling about that." Second it's helped me learn human anatomy and physiology. Third, because Usui Reiki promotes intuition, it's helped me learn to trust my instincts and intuition. And lastly Usui Reiki has helped me tune into the part of myself that desires to help people. Martial art is all about protecting others and ourselves from harm. Usui Reiki constantly reminds me that my role as a warrior is not to do others harm, but rather to only use force to protect myself and others from harm.

Are we truly training like warriors?
May 2011
Monthly Student Newsletter

Since leaving my career in law enforcement I've been struggling with the idea of being a full time private trainer and martial arts instructor. I wasn't quite sure what that should look like. During my first month after quitting the Alberta Sheriffs Dept. I watched a lot of television as I asked myself, "What is it I'm supposed to be doing." I recently found someone who helped me find the answer.

I found my answer in the most unlikely of places, yoga. FTS has recently partnered with Body Soul Connexions, a wellness company in Okotoks AB. The owner and primary instructor H.F. shared with me her training regime and schedule. She trains most weeks 7 days a week, minimum 5. When she's not training or teaching in the formal sense she's researching, writing, and thinking about training. She promotes healthy living and sets a high standard for herself in terms of diet and exercise. Sometimes when she's at home doing daily chores she'll drop into a pose, or use chores and work as extra exercise. She walks, runs, and rides her bike regularly. Some days she's up as early as 5am to train. Sometimes she goes away for 6 week intensives where her sleep, training, and diet are strictly regulated so that her skills can advance to the next level.

The more she shared with me her training routine the more I questioned how often we, as warriors, or worse as warrior trainers, could keep up with that routine. Often we say that we train in the warrior arts, or we train others to be warriors. Yet we eat crap food, don't regulate our sleep or manage our stress appropriately, don't go to the gym, skip training classes, and don't really apply ourselves while we are training. We go to training conferences and use it as an excuse to drink to excess and miss classes the next day and we laugh about it. Then when we teach recruits or students we use terms like "live the warrior lifestyle", "follow the warrior code", and "take care of yourselves 'cuz it's a tough role." Well I can assure you, we don't train, or act, the way warriors used to.

We look at the sensationalism of warrior cultures, the Spartans, the Samurai, Ninja, Paladins, and countless others, yet we fail to realize these warriors trained to the point of exhaustion daily for their entire lives. They would laugh at 99% of us if they saw how we "train." We create conditions so safe that there's hardly any contact, no chance of a trip slip or fall, we are afraid to move because we might get hurt, or be sore the next day. We skip classes and workouts regularly because "I'm tired, I don't want to, I don't feel like it." We wonder why most professional warriors, and even a large percentage of warrior trainers, are overweight. We refuse to invest into ourselves, complain when our employer doesn't take care of us, or want our instructors to motivate, encourage, and push us.

And yet people who do yoga, an activity that doesn't prepare you for life or death conflicts, an activity that for the most part is recreational and therapeutic, are up at 5am training 1,2, 3 times a day, 5-7days a week. Yet trying to get a martial arts student to commit to 3- 90min classes per week is like pulling teeth. Am I the only one that sees something wrong with this picture?

I didn't tell her I was writing this article so out of respect for her privacy I won't use her name, but thank you H.F. for the inspiration and for showing me what it means to be a professional. I for one am getting off my butt, no more excuses for missing class or workouts, no more eating junk and trying to justify it to myself, no more abusing training and learning opportunities as excuses to destroy my body. For years I've thought of myself as a warrior, but wasn't really applying myself to that standard. I urge all of you to evaluate your training and ask yourself who's more of a warrior? You, for all your talk and lip service, or the H.F.'s of the world who are truly taking their craft seriously?

The Chakra's of Reiki
August 2011
Combat Network Magazine

Last month you were introduced to Reiki, the Japanese system of using universal life energy to heal emotional and physical ailments. Recall that Reiki translated means Spirit Energy and is the practice of "laying on hands" where the Reiki Master focus' the energy through the 7 chakra's to remove spiritual blockages. A blockage in each of the chakras will manifest in various physical symptoms.

Each Chakra is thought to be a vortex of energy that allows Reiki to flow and is located at a position in the body.

The 7 Chakra's

Chakra #1. Sahasrara the Crown Chakra. The Crown Chakra is located above the crown of the head and is represented by a symbol of a thousand pedal purple lotus. Physically it's connected to the central nervous system, the hypothalamus, and the pituitary gland. A blockage or damage to the Sahasrara can manifest itself in health problems related to skeletal muscle, skin, and central nervous system ailments such as headaches and dizziness.

Chakra #2. Ajna the Third Eye. Ajna is located in the middle of the forehead between the eyes. It is represented by a two pedal indigo lotus. It is linked to the pineal gland and pituitary gland as well as the eyes, ears, brain, nose, and central nervous system. Physical ailments include difficulty sleeping (due to irregular melatonin secretion), nose and sinus problems, neurological disorders, stroke, brain tumor, seizures and spinal issues.

Chakra #3. Vishuddha the Throat Chakra. The Throat Chakra is located right in the throat and represented by white crescent in the middle of turquoise pedals. This Chakra is primarily related to the thyroid, neck, teeth, gums, jaw, and muscles. Raspy throat, chronic soar throat, mouth ulcers, gum difficulties, scoliosis, laryngitis, swollen glands, thyroid problems, headaches, pain in the neck and shoulders, ear infections and problems.

Chakra #4. Anahata the Heart Chakra. Anahata is symbolized by a green flower with 12 pedals and is related to the thymus, endocrine system, and immune system. Specific organs include the heart, the lungs, the upper back, the skin, the shoulders and arms, the diaphragm, and the immune system. Asthma, allergies, circulation problems, and tension in the shoulder blades can all be indicators that there is a problem with the Heart Chakra.

Chakra #5. Manipura the Solar Plexus Chakra. Manipura is related to the pancreas, the adrenal glands, and the adrenal cortex, and the digestive system. It is represented by a upside down triangle with ten yellow pedals. Disease and symptoms' include anything to do with the digestive system and it's components, lower back, and the sympathetic nervous system.

Chakra #6. Swadhisthana the Sacral Chakra. The Sacral Chakra is represented by a crescent moon surrounded orange by 6 pedals and is related to the reproductive organs, the lower vertebrae, hips, prostate, lymphatic system, and all body fluids. Dysfunctions of the reproductive organs or disease, issues with the spleen, urinary system, or loss of appetite, sexual appetite, sciatica pain and lower back pain can all be associated to this Chakra.

Chakra #7. Muladhara the Root Chakra. Muladhara is located at the perineum and represented by 5 red rose pedals. Legs, feet, bone and marrow, rectum, and the base of the spine are all associated to the Root Chakra. Disorders with the legs and feet as well as bowels, large intestines, eating disorders, chronic lower back pain, and immune system diseases can all be accredited to this chakra.

If you have any of the ailments associated with the Chakra's as listed above Reiki may help. A Reiki treatment can help clear blockages and heal the body parts and systems associated with the Chakra. A Reiki treatment can be focused on a specific Chakra if a patient is representing specific ailments or a general treatment can be used. Remember that the Reiki energy will travel through the Chakra's healing any that require it and promote specific body and emotional health.

The Kihon Happo, The Kata of the Bujinkan
September 2011
Combat Network Magazine

In last months article you were introduced to Bujinkan Budo Taijutsu, the proper name for what's commonly referred to as Ninjutsu. Remember that Bujinkan Budo Taijutsu is built out of components of 9 traditional Japanese martial arts schools. Just like every traditional school those 9 had forms, or scripted patterns referred to as Kata, for students to learn the basic techniques of the school. This does not mean however that the Bujinkan kata are comprised of all the kata of the 9 schools.

Instead Hatsumi Sensei, the creator and current soke of the Bujinkan, created a system of 8 techniques referred to as the Kihon Happo. Kihon Happo loosely translates as "Basics of Life." This is significant in that it indicates to Bujinkan students that Hatsumi Sensei is transmitting to us that this is the base of all body mechanics used in the Bujinkan.
Techniques of the Kata

The Kihon Happo is comprised of 8 techniques and 1 throw. Throughout the 9 techniques in the form the Tori demonstrates 6 Ju Jutsu (grappling) Techniques and 3 Dakentaijutsu (long form striking) techniques.

The kata starts with a series of wrist locks from a high lapel grab. Uda Gyaku, and Omote Gyaku are demonstrated along with a high block in the 3rd form. Next 3 long form striking (Dakentaijutsu) techniques. Ichimonji no kamae kihon happo starts with the Tori and Uke facing each other in Ichimonji no kamae and utilizes a high block to defend a straight punch and a downwards Shuto (knife hand) strike to the attackers collar bone. Next Jumonji no kamae kihon happo utilizes rear angular movement and high blocks as well as strategic striking to manipulate the attackers balance. The 2nd technique, Hicho no kamae kihon happo, uses the Rising Crane posture with a low block to defend an attack to the stomach as well as a toe kick under the attackers arm pit and strategic striking to manipulate balance.

After technique number 3 the 2 major arm breaking techniques are taught. Oni kidaki (Breaking the Demon) and musha dori (Empty Hand Defense) both utilize various arm wrapping techniques to break the attackers arm at the elbow and shoulder. Both also teach how to use an attackers arm to manipulate balance and take the attacker down (koppo jutsu). Finally Gansaki Nage (Throwing the Big Stone) is taught. Most schools teach Gansaki Nage at the end of the Kihon Happo but don't consider it to actually be part of the kata.

The 9 techniques briefly described above teach all of the basic postures (kamae), most of the basic strikes, concepts of skeletal manipulation (Koppo Jutsu) and pressure point strikes (Koshi Jutsu). These are the basic elements of the Bujinkan martial arts system.

Moving Past the Basics

Once a student as demonstrated proficiency in the Kihon Happo they then attempt to develop 8 variations (Henka) for EACH of the 8 techniques in the Kihon Happo. Once they are successful in developing 64 Henka then they are tasked with developing another 8 variations on each of the new techniques and so on. This results in a kata with an infinite number of variations.

This is truly the spirit of Bujinkan Budo Taijutsu. Freedom of destructive movement that utilizes basic positions and methods of striking and grappling to create a whole system. There are so many henka on the Kihon Happo now sometimes it can be difficult to find an instructor that knows the kata the way it's meant to be taught and passed on to students.

The River of Life
September 2011
Monthly Student Newsletter

Just about a year ago I had an opportunity to write an article for new police officers. The purpose of the book that the article was going into was to provide new officers with tips on what to expect during their career. It was a project being undertaken by Brian Willis and the book is titles "If I Knew Then." Unfortunately I didn't complete the article by the deadline and it's not in the book but through the process of writing it I changed the way I see life so I'd like to share it with you.

Shortly before writing the article I was at a training intensive hosted by Shihan Jay Creasey. As part of the training we did some white water rafting and rescue. The point of the exercise was to explore the river to teach us about the importance of flow in our martial arts technique. Our guide Derek Holmes said something that I found very powerful during the exercise. "You don't conquer a river; she just lets you play in her for awhile." The concepts these two men taught over the weekend influenced how I see the world around me now.

I used to see parts of my life as being separate from each other. I used to see my relationships separate from my work which was separate from my martial arts which was separate from my interest in health and on and on and on. Now however I see every part of my life complimenting the rest. There is no separation between the areas of my life, they've all flowed together to be part of the same river of life.

Just like a river has a certain flow rate, our life has a certain flow rate. Where a river is measured in cubic meters per second, our lives are measured in seconds. Each second is the exact same length as the one before it and the one after it, but yet they can feel very different. Just like the flow rate of water can be the same at different sections but depending on the section that flow rate can be experienced very differently. Depending on what's happing to us a second may seem frozen in time for an eternity, or it may be so inconsequential that we don't even notice it's passed.

When navigating a river you have to be very much aware of the moment. If you're thinking too much about what's ahead, or what you just passed, you might make a mistake with severe consequences. Just like in life we should be very much in the moment. If we're concerned with the past, or looking too far to the future, we may miss important things in the present.

Rivers are described as flowing to a destination, not away from one. This is important for our own lives, that we see ourselves working towards things, not running away from what's behind us. But where does our life flow to? In the words of sensei Raphael from Take Dojo, "We live, we procreate, we die. That is all." All of our lives are flowing in the same direction, towards an eventual end. But just like a good white water river navigator prepares to ride the flow of the river knowing that eventually that river will terminate, so too should we prepare to ride the flow of life knowing that eventually it will terminate.

Since seeing my life this way I've been able to obtain a new level of confidence. That confidence comes with knowing that my life is flowing forwards. And that just because something's happening at this bend of the river, a change of scenery is right around the next bend. All I have to do is navigate my way there. To steal Derek's quote, you can't conquer life, she just lets you play in her for awhile.

Pay Now or Pay Later….. With Interest
October 2011
Monthly Student Newsletter

Generally speaking in the FTS Newsletters I write 3 articles. One designed to encourage and inspire different budo values, one geared towards law enforcement, and one addressing health and wellness. This month is a little different; this one article addresses all three. I hope you enjoy it.

Recently at Foothills Training Services I've expanded the programs we deliver. In the Martial Arts Division I've added a Tuesday night general martial arts and combatives class led by Sifu Kevin Goat, and I've added an Arnis De Cadena/Balintawak Eskrima class once per month. In the Tactical Division I've added St. John's ambulance first aid and CPR taught by Karla Cote, and in the Health and Wellness division we offer Self Hypnosis, Positive Self Talk, Healthy Living, as well as Fitness and Nutrition Consultation, Massage, Reiki, and Hypnotherapy. We also regularly have Self Defense that runs for members of class or the community.

The reason why I provide so many different programs and services are that I truly believe in the "pay now, or pay later" saying. What do I mean? I mean that often we pass on classes or information that could really benefit our lives. Sometimes by doing so we pass up training, education, and knowledge that could make a big difference in our lives. Sometimes later on in life we end up in situations where, had we attended that class days, weeks, months, or years ago we wouldn't be here now. This newsletter goes out to nearly 600 people every month. The information in it is current and accurate, and free! Many of our classes are below market value, some of them are free to attend or $10/hour. Yet what blows me away for the last 4 years is how many people don't attend the sessions. Generally speaking only about 100 people will open this newsletter. Fewer will read its entire contents. Even though I provide up to date information for free to other martial artists, health practitioners, and law enforcement professionals every month about 1% of people will remove themselves from the mailing list.

There are excellent reasons to not attend training, but there's also some excuses, and some ignorance. Usually I would let people decide for themselves what to attend and what not too and that it's not my place to push them. But the more I think about the world around us the more I've decided it's part of my job to educate. That's my occupation and my duty. So here's the brutal honesty.

You can pay now, or you can pay later, with interest. What does that even mean? Well it means that I heard three common responses to why people didn't look into the classes or register. The first was that they didn't need the information. The second was that they couldn't afford the training. And the third was that they had previously attended the class or something similar. Does this sound like you? Do these reasons sound like good reasons to not attend? I'm going to tell you they aren't.

The two classes I push the most are first aid/CPR and self defense. Both of these classes focus on hard skills (that is skills that are physical in nature and deteriorate without use and practice), and both classes focus on emergency situations where the training can make the difference between injury or death, or safety.

The number one response from people for not attending the First Aid/CPR class is, "my work doesn't require me to have it." Well pardon my language but screw your work. Who cares if your work requires you to have it? What about your family, your friends, the stranger you're going to come across who's hurt and is looking to anyone for help? How about yourself when you get hurt and there's no one around to help you? Do you know what to do when that kid at the table next to yours in the restaurant is choking? How about when you're on family vacation and the car in front of you loses control, gets in a collision, and there's blood, glass, metal, and frightened people all around you? Will you know what to do? You might think you do but ask yourself honestly, "am I prepared for a first aid emergency? If I need help or someone I care about needs help do I have the knowledge and skills to do it?"

The second class I really try to get people into is the self protection class. The number one reason for not attending that class was along the lines of "it's not going to happen to me." I can understand people thinking that. We live in a civilized part of the world. Many of the people I ask aren't party animals who live a high risk lifestyle. Many of them have families and when they travel it's to resorts or hotels or tourist destinations. On the face of it seems like a pretty safe lifestyle. But look deeper.

I'm sure the 10 tourists killed in Mexico last year didn't think it would happen to them. I sure didn't think 3 men would want to hospitalize me or worse over a parking spot 5 years ago. I'm sure the girls in Canadian universities and colleges who are sexually assaulted every year don't think it'll happen to them. I'm sure the fathers and sons suddenly caught in the Vancouver riots in June didn't think they'd ever need self protection training. How about an extreme example, the people on the airlines on September 11, 2001. Did they ever think a plane they were on would get hijacked? Would you? Here's a better question, if you're in any of these situations do you know what to do? Would you know how to protect yourself, your spouse, your parents, your kids, your grandparents, your friends?

So let's look at reason number 2. "I can't afford the training." This is my favorite all time reason not to attend a class because it's almost always followed two weeks later with, "hey do you want to go out drinking tonight?" You can afford the training so stop pretending you can't. And if you truly can't and want to attend come talk to me, I will never let finances stop a student from attending a course I'm involved with. NEVER. I especially love this reason for the health and wellness seminars or classes. What people don't realize is that if they follow the information contained in those seminars it could save them hundreds or even thousands of dollars in treatments and prescriptions years down the road. If I offered you a chance to invest $50 today, and in 15 years it has the potential to mature to over $10000 would you invest? Pay now, or pay later, with interest.

And reason number 3, "I took that course already." This is the number one reason police officers and security guards don't come back for regular training. I know you took it already, months or years ago. This is like a pro quarterback coming back to training camp after break and saying to the coach, "but I threw the football last year so I already know how so I don't need to train." It's absolutely ridiculous. Do you really think the skills you practiced for 4 hours a year ago will still be there for you when you need them in a rapidly deteriorating chaotic situation? Probably not.

So to get to the point I've identified 4 areas that you should seek regular information in. You should be willing to invest some time, effort, and money today into these areas because it could pay dividends down the road. If you don't invest into these areas you might be ok. You also might get sick, get hurt, get someone else hurt, or not be able to take care of yourself or the people you care about when the time comes. The 4 areas are Health and Wellness (including mental and physical), Self Protection and Self Defense, First Aid and CPR, and Emergency Preparedness. There are other ways to prepare for those things other than attending my courses. There are other courses available, information online and in books and other professional services from different professions.

But do one thing for me, for yourself, for your friends and loved ones. If you've had the blinders on until now, please take them off and invest into yourself. Pay a little in terms of money, time, resources, and discomfort now so that when the time comes down the road you need it you have it and you won't have to pay then. The interest I keep talking about should be straight forward by now. It's the potential for things to be way worse. For sickness to be more devastating, pain to be greater, injury to be more severe, and loss of life more a tragedy. That's the interest you're risking if you don't make the investment now. And if you have already I thank you. If ever I need help it's a great feeling knowing there are people out there I can turn to with the skills required.

Living the life of a healthy warrior
February 2012
ILEETA Journal

The Problem

Law enforcement comes with a variety of health issues that are exclusive to the occupation, but rather are common to it. These issues may be physical or mental and can vary from diabetes, chronic shoulder or back pain, sleep disorders, high blood pressure, depression, anxiety, to a host of many others.

Often we train to "win the fight" or to "rule the night." We think of this as training for that ultimate test or our skill and resolve, a lethal force encounter. In focusing on that low probability-high impact event are we losing sight of other areas of our health and wellness that we affect our everyday lives? After all, what good is winning a gun fight if 15 years later you can't hug your children or grandchildren due to chronic illness, pain, or disease?

I'm not suggesting that training to win an encounter with an assailant isn't important or can be ignored. I am suggesting however that in addition it's time to focus on overall wellness as Warriors. This overall wellness can be achieved by focusing on 3 major systems of the body and their health. They are Gut Health, Central Nervous System Health, and Mental/Emotional Health.

The goal of this article is to teach you simple methods to get these 3 systems performing optimally again without the need for surgery or prescriptions.

Gut Health

Gut health refers to the health of the digestive system and all its components. These include the stomach, pancreas, gall bladder, intestines, and waste removal organs. If the digestive system isn't performing nutrients aren't making their way into the body. This can result in organ failure and disease. An unhealthy digestive system can lead to diabetes, stones, acid reflux, inflammation of muscles, joint pain in the skeletal system, difficulty focusing or concentrating, build up of toxins, high blood sugar, obesity, high blood pressure, high cholesterol, heart attack, stroke, and a host of other diseases. Poor and toxic diet is also believed to be a contributing factor in the onset of cancer.

There are two major causes of poor gut health. The first is stress. When humans are under stress the brain diverts blood away from the digestive system. Often officers are consuming food while under stress. This means that the system does not have the resources to digest the food ingested. Even if the food can be broken down it doesn't mean that the nutrients are being used in an optimal way.

The second major cause of poor gut health is consumption of bad food. The North American diet is leading to a growing number of adults and youth being overweight and/or obese. Fast food, sugary food, high energy food, foods loaded with fat, and a belief that it's our right to consume large quantities all contribute to us having junk in our guts. As the saying goes, "garbage in, garbage out." We cannot expect to have a healthy digestive system if all we're ever putting in it is junk. Often our over reliance on over the counter medications or supplements as well as prescription drugs can lead to poor gut health. Many of these drugs or supplements are very hard on the digestive system and can leave it damaged and not operating as it was intended.

Central Nervous System Health

The Central Nervous System (CNS) is mainly comprised of the brain, spine, and nerves. It can be damaged due to impact, injury, trauma, poor posture, poor food consumption, and a lack of fitness. When the central nervous system becomes damaged it affects every other system and organ in the body. If messages from the brain aren't received by the rest of the body the organ(s) won't function optimally. This can result in disease in the organ or other system, even though the cause is in the CNS.

When asked a physician will treat the site where the damage or disease is apparent, often overlooking the CNS as the cause of the disease. Likewise damage to the CNS can manifest itself as mental health diseases such as depression and anxiety.

Often people think that because they don't have pain in the head or spine that everything is fine. Often however an unhealthy CNS will not produce any pain in the head or spine until 5-10 years after the damage or injury was caused. When people do start to feel pain in the form of back pain or headaches they often reach for a pill to make the discomfort and pain go away. This doesn't fix the problem however and may actually make it worse. As well those pills often have a negative effect on Gut Health.

Mental/Emotional Health

Mental and Emotional Health is the product of 2 different systems. First Mental Health (or unhealthy as it were) may be a by product of the functioning of the Brain. It may also be however how the Mind interprets our environment. It is possible to have a properly functioning brain but still develop Mental or Emotional Health problems.

Often these problems can result in deterioration of relationships, both professional and personal, poor work performance, and a compromised quality of living. In extreme cases they can cause to domestically abuse their partners or children or worse to take their own lives even murder another.

The most common Emotional Health problem for LEO's is Post Traumatic Stress Syndrome, Depression, and Anxiety. Sometimes officers have been living with these for so long they don't even realize they're sick.

The Solutions

Nutrition

It surprises me how easy it is to fall for bad nutrition due to media marketing. Take for example some fast food restaurants. Many now offer deli sandwiches on their "Healthy" menu. Many of these deli sandwiches have more simple carbohydrates and fat then do the fast burger options! Most muffins at delicatessens or cafés are marketed as being a healthy alternative but in reality they have more sugar and calories then do donuts. The point is this; you may think you're making healthy choices when you're not even close.

Break the types of foods down into their major categories. They are; Dairy, Meats, Fruits and Vegetables, and Grains. Everyday make it a point to consume a certain number of servings of each. For dairy have 3 servings, 8 of fruits or vegetables , 3 of meats, and 5 of grains.

Now start looking at the types of each. For example Almond milk falls into the dairy category and is better for you then animal milk or soy milk. Almond milk helps regulate stomach PH which will result in foods digesting better. Yogurts that are high in vitamins and calcium as well as pro biotics will help your stomach and body also.

Refined grains are bad for you, especially on night shift. Due to hormonal changes at night the more simple the carbohydrate the more likely it is to be stored as fat. Whole grains are your ally. Avoid sugar and substitutes and any white starch such as regular pasta, white bread, baking, and potatoes. This means get the sugar out of the coffee and use honey instead. While you're at it eliminate the cream and use milk. Healthy granola and oatmeal's can be convenient when in a rush.

Attempt to eat more vegetables then fruit and use berries to add flavor to your meals. Berries are rich in antioxidants and micro nutrients and can help make meals more flavorful, especially yogurt and salads. Vegetables should be rich in colour. The more colourful the more nutrients. Spinach, bell peppers, purple onion, tomatoes, and peas are all excellent choices.

Try to avoid red meat. Instead substitute fish, chicken, and eggs. Eggs and fish especially contain omega fatty acids and will help your body tremendously, especially in a combative situation. Red meats are higher in fats and cholesterol.

Next take these serving suggestions and understand when to eat them. When you first wake up grains and fruits are best to kick start the body and provide fuel to get going. As your day progresses meats and vegetables should be increased and grains and fruits decreased. This provides you a lean energy source and one that will be long burning incase of an emergency situation. Break your servings into 3 larger meals and 3 mini meals between them. Don't eat any more then 1 serving of meat in a sitting. Also don't consume fluids before eating meat, instead save your drink for after.

Find time to relax before ingesting your meals. Food eaten while rushed results in the stomach having to do more work then it's intended because portions aren't chewed enough, as well means that it's trying to digest food while the brain is diverting blood elsewhere. Even 10 deep breaths can make a huge difference in what happens to your food once it's past your face.

Every 6 months take a round of over the counter pro biotics. I know you think that you're getting enough in your yogurt but it's a marketing ploy. Do to poor food, medications, and stress the stomach likely requires a pro biotic boost every 6 months.

Vitamin B supplements are excellent for combating cortisol due to sleep irregularities and stress and a good multivitamin supplement can go a long ways in overall health.

The last part of the equation is hydration. Consume no less than 2 liters of water per day. Aim for 4 liters per day. Watch the caffeine consumption. It dehydrates you and is hard on the stomach. Water should be filtered for maximum effectiveness. Also avoid energy drinks, the amount of sugar, caffeine, and other compounds are very toxic.

Fitness

As officers experience stress and hypervigilance throughout their shift stress chemicals all build up in the body. The primary of these chemicals of course being adrenalin. These chemicals can be corrosive to nerves and muscle if not removed. The only way to remove most of them is through activity. For this reason it is best to exercise shortly after your shift. Exercising after work has been found to have a dramatic affect on officers' attitudes and energy levels at home also. After all what good is saving the streets if your negative attitude breaks your families' heart every time you walk in the door?

So what kind of fitness is best? In short the answer is Combat Fitness. Combat Fitness is fitness that focus' on Power, Speed, Endurance, Flexibility, Balance, and Energy System Recovery. These fitness routines are short and high intensity. They burn off stress chemicals, strengthen the body and aid in proper alignment of head and spine, decrease body fat and increase lean muscle, improve cardio vascular health, and prepare officers for an assaultive encounter. Sounds pretty good doesn't it? There are several different programs available including P90X, Insanity, and Crossfit. Consult qualified trainers before going too intense and hurting yourself.

Post workout is the best time to consume anything that's high in sugar. If done correctly a high intensity fitness routine will result in the depletion of body sugars. Your body needs sugar to survive. By eating healthy sugars post workout you can ensure that they are going to rebuild muscle and not store as fat deposits.

Mental Exercise

The stress of working in law enforcement can lead to poor posture due to muscle tension, anxiety, depression, hostility, digestive issues, and the deterioration of relationships. There's a reason why nearly ½ of all North American marriages result in divorce.

Proper nutrition and fitness will go a long ways in helping mental and emotional health. The problem is though which comes first, the chicken or the egg? Does physical health deteriorate emotional health or is it the other way around? If you're tackling both does it matter?

Mental exercise can result in lower levels of stress chemicals which can drastically affect CNS and Gut Health. This combined with proper nutrition and fitness is a powerful recipe for success.

There are various mental exercises' you can engage in. I recommend 3 for the officer who's new to this concept. The first is relaxation exercises. The easiest one of these is auto-genic training. To perform these exercises simply find a quiet place to sit or lie down. Begin breathing deeply. Every exhalation count a number from 1-10. When you reach 10 start back at 1. If you notice other thoughts then the numbers start back at 1. If you notice you've lost count or gone over 10 start back at one. Perform for 5 minutes a day every day.

The second Mental Exercise if recommend is Yoga, Tai Chi, Qi Gong, or and stretching routine. Stretching is a very relaxing activity and tackles one of the core elements of combat fitness, flexibility. I recommend stretching routines that particularly focus on back and spine health. This way your CNS Health will benefit also.

The 3rd type of Mental Exercise is Imagery (not visualization). Again find a safe and quiet place and close your eyes. Perform a few cycles of deep breathing. Allow yourself to Imagine peaceful and successful situations

These 3 Mental Exercises will decrease stress, lower stress hormones, improve muscle function and posture, and increase blood flow to the digestive system.

Chiropractic

For various reasons the spine may be out of alignment. A professional chiropractor will work with you to make adjustments to the spine in a variety of ways. Once these adjustments are made pressure comes off the spinal cord and neurotransmissions flow uninterrupted from the brain to the organs. These results in optimal organ and system function. Combined with nutrition, fitness, and mental exercise, Chiropractic can help restore the body to its natural optimal state.

Conclusion

The body is designed to regulate and heal itself. Most physicians agree that surgeries and medications would not be necessary for most people if healthier life choices were made. Following these guidelines won't make you invincible or mean that you'll never need a prescription or procedure. What they do is increase your quality of life and make you more whole Physically and Emotionally.

If you're already on prescription medications begin following these guidelines and start working with your family doctor to get off the drugs. Prescriptions aren't designed to fix very many problems, instead they allow you to live with them. Instead try returning to a state of health. In my experience within 6-12 months many people are able to begin coming off prescriptions that doctors originally thought they'd need the rest of their lives.

These suggestions take time and effort. In the beginning it may be difficult. You might cheat once in awhile or not follow them. That's ok, nobody's perfect. You will need a warriors discipline to make these changes part of your life, but in the end it's worth it. You have the power to make a choice. To invest some time, effort, and maybe money into your health now, or to pay later, with interest. Which will you choose?

Feeling Intent
March 2012
Combat Network Magazine

In previous articles I outlined what Reiki is and how Reiki is used to clear Chakra's to help heal and aid physical ailments and disease. This article will discuss Aura, what it is, how it works, and how a martial artist can use it to their advantage.

Remember that Reiki is an energy that moves through from our crown chakra above our heads, down through our body, and out the root chakra below our pelvis connecting us with the earth. Our *Aura* is related to Reiki in that it's the energy we give off out to the rest of the world. Think of this energy like ripples in a pond radiating out from the center.

Many spiritual leaders from around the world and from a variety of religious faiths report being able to see people's aura and that provides them insight into the person's character and thoughts. In many paintings Jesus Christ is depicted with an aura radiating around his head. The colours of the Buddhist flags represent the colours of each layer of the aura and Islamic traditions make mention of energy, aura's, and bodies of light surrounding individuals.

In the book The Book of Six Rings, author, psychic, and martial artist Jock Brocas explains how being sensitive to an attackers *Aura* allows a martial artist to detect when an attack is imminent and move before the attacker does. Have you ever been in the presence of another person and got a very uneasy feeling? Felt anxiety from someone you didn't know? Or just can't put your finger on why you don't care for a certain person although they've never done anything to you? This can all be explained by the concept of aura.

Because auras are the energy we put off to the rest of the world they are changed by our thoughts, feelings, intent, and emotions. Just like the ripples in a pond will change depending on what's been dropped into the water so too will our auras change depending on what we're thinking and feeling. If for example an attacker is thinking about hurting someone, then their aura will change with that thought. The more intense the thought the greater the shift in their aura. The reverse of this is that if someone truly cares about you and is thinking about your well being and emotionally concerned for you their aura will change.

This is one of the reasons why it's critical in martial arts training to train with intent and not just go through the motions. Training with intent allows training partners to become sensitive to these shifts in aura even if you can't *see* them you can *feel* them. It's through developing this sensitivity that allows people to develop their *sixth sense*, or their *intuition*. The more sensitive you get to feeling these shifts in aura the more likely you are to feel them even if you're not in the immediate presence of the other person. Other factors that may affect this are your relationship to the person and the intensity of the thought or emotion.

It's also important to develop a state of thoughtlessness in your training to help you hide your true intent from an opponent. Learning to conceal your aura, your intent, and your energy is just as critical as becoming sensitive to other people's.

Stephen Hayes has published some good drills and exercises throughout the year to help martial arts students become sensitive to auras around them. Try this exercise; sit or stand relaxed with your eyes closed and seek a state of thoughtlessness and an empty mind. Have your training partner stand in front of you and when they're ready begin thinking intensely violent thoughts about you. Raise your hand when you feel like something's not right. Once you've experienced some success with that add another training partner and now one thinks violent thoughts about you and imagines doing violence to you and the other thinks positive thoughts about you. Raise your arm that corresponds with the negative feelings. If you can experience some success with these exercises then you are becoming sensitive to feeling the auras of other people around you.

Getting a 2-for-1
April 2012
Monthly Student Newsletter

     Law Enforcement trainers know that many officers do not have the time, money, space, or other resources to adequately practice and train their skills. They also are keenly aware that the majority of agencies do not provide enough training time or hours annually to prepare officers to the degree that trainers would like them prepared. More and more officers are taking responsibility for their own health and fitness however. How, as a training officer, can you capitalize on utilizing physical exercise routines to develop combative or control tactics skills?

     Nearly every technique or skill has a one-person drill that can be done to develop it, or a combination of skills. Once these drills can be isolated they can be added into a physical fitness routine as either a warm up or in the case of surge style training an exercise station. By combining their technical drills into a work out offices can get twice as much benefit out of their time. By combining drills into their work outs officers can achieve a 2-for-1 workout. Below I'll provide some examples for consideration. If you're not familiar with the drills or techniques consider seeking professional instruction.

     Ground fighting is one of the most intense encounters an officer can face on duty. Ground fights are down and dirty, limit the chance for disengagement, increase energy expenditure, and decrease an officer's ability to generate force in strikes or access weapons. This is an excellent area to drill during exercise to increase the chance of victory. Wrestling and Brazilian Jiu-Jitsu coaches discovered this a long time ago and have already done the work for you and created hundreds of high intensity skill enhancing exercises and drills. The first of these drills is the "bridge." The bridge is completed by laying flat on your back, feet tucked in, arching as high as you can with your shoulders on the ground, and reaching across your body with one hand thereby rotating your hips and shoulders.

The second of these exercises is the "sprawl." This is completed from a standing position by putting your hands on the ground between your feet, kicking your legs out behind you and pressing your pelvis into the floor while arching your back and looking up. For added intensity use this as a burpie variation.

The third movement comes from wrestling and is referred to as "break dancing." It's somewhat complicated but to start adopt a position on your hands and knees. Shift your weight to one side and bring the opposite hand off the floor and put that same side foot on the floor. Kick your opposite leg underneath and out in front of you and sit on your outside cheek. Reset to center and repeat on the other side.

The last drill for skill enhancement exercise is the "shrimp." Lay flat on you back, feet tucked in close. Arch your back slightly and extend your legs as you push your rear out to one side and turn to face the opposite side. Finish the movement by curling in and reaching for your toes with your hands.

These are just four examples of Wrestling and BJJ drills that can be both physically demanding and will enhance ground fighting skills. Possible workout combinations are endless but to get started take the 4 exercises, perform each one for 90 seconds with intensity, take a one minute break and repeat twice more. For added intensity jump into the air at the end of a sprawl to turn it into a burpie.

Enjoy the workout and as always, stay safe and be well.

Shuriken Jutsu The Art of the Throwing Blade
June 2012
Combat Network Magazine

One of the most iconic images of Japans mysterious warrior, the ninja, is the throwing star. After all, what ninja movie would be complete without hundreds of throwing stars being launched throughout the movie cutting down any opponent in their path? Just like most things in ninja movies however, this image and the modern depiction of throwing stars isn't entirely accurate.

Let us begin by looking at the term, "shuriken jutsu." In this case the word "shu" means "hand", "ri" means "release", and "ken" means "blade." If you recall from my previous articles "jutsu" means "a system of offensive and defensive techniques", usually shortened to the "art" of something. Therefore "shuriken jutsu" can be defined as "the art of the hand released blade." Shuriken jutsu isn't unique to the ninja. In Japan alone many other martial art schools explored how to throw various blades including Samurai schools. *Miyamoto Musashi*, perhaps the most famous Japanese swords master in history, developed and taught techniques for throwing his Katana and Wakizashi.

Throwing stars are attributed to ***Togakure-ryū*** Ninpo School. This is thought to be the oldest form of Ninjutsu still taught today and focused on a particular mindset more than techniques to win a fight. In the ***Togakure-ryū*** many of the beginner level kata's focus on launching either a shuriken or blinding powder at the opponent. ***Togakure-ryū*** means hidden door school and was created as a school to counter samurai who excelled at using swords, spears, and bow and arrow. One of the focus' of the ***Togakure-ryū*** is concealment of armour, weapons, ability, and intent.

The throwing stars from **Togakure-ryū** are referred to as "Senban Shuriken" which is a name given to them to distinguish their shape and construction. Senban were nail removers and were modified to be used as throwing weapons. There are many other shapes of throwing stars however, including Bo Shuriken which essentially means "Staff Hand Released Blade" and resembles a spike, and Tanto Shuriken which is a throwing knife.

These throwing weapons resemble modern variations in shape only. The size and weight have changed drastically over the years. The two critical factors to do tissue damage from any strike or striking object are mass and velocity (kinetic energy=mass X velocity (acceleration)). The warriors and soldiers that depended on these weapons for their safety wee very aware of this fact. Senban shuriken measured approximately 1 hand width across and could've weighted up to 1 pound. Bo Shuriken were the length of a forearm and up to 5mm thick. They were usually pointed on both ends and both were kept concealed in pockets against the torso or along the forearms where they could be used to deflect blows and swords. Tanto Shuriken were concealed in boots with the blades facing out towards the front of the shin and could deliver extra damage when "cut kicks" were used. The reason for the size and weight of the weapon was therefore double duty, to use as a defense and type of body armour, and to deliver more kinetic energy when thrown for greater tissue damage and wounds and to help penetrate light armour.

Shuriken weren't always used to throw at and hurt and opponent. They could be used to cause distractions by launching into the grass or trees to make noise where a Ninja wanted opponent's to go to, or they could be coated in oil and set on fire and thrown into buildings, barns, people, and grass or bushes. All types of shuriken were also held onto by the warrior using them and used as a hand held weapon to cut, puncture, or trap with. Generally though they were used to distract a pursuer or attacker and were launched in volleys'. The movie image of a small piece of shiny silver steel travelling through three walls and a car door to strike an opponent in the throat and kill them just isn't realistic. Thrown in multiples at an opponent's head, neck, and chest however as they're chasing you through a dark forest could be enough to cause serious injury, or at least psychologically persuade the pursuer to not continue the chase.

There are several methods to throw Shuriken at a target but for the purpose of this article I'll only illustrate the three most effective methods. Remember that once launched the blade will rotate through the air. For this reason 4 pointed (or more) stars are most effective because if the throwers range to the target doesn't allow for complete rotations one or more points will still strike. In the case of Bo Shuriken or Tanto Shuriken however the thrower must take the range to the target into account and calculate how many rotations the weapon will make while in flight to the target.

For the first technique hold the blade in your dominant hand by pinching it between the thumb and forefinger. Stand with your dominant leg back. Take one full step forward as you raise your hand straight up from the shoulder over your head. As your foot lands drop your arm with power and when your hand is pointing directly at your target let of the projectile. Adjust range for the rotations of the weapon. The second technique is starts the same way but this time only half step so that your dominant foot is even with your support foot. Step back with the support foot to generate power and follow the same arm movement as before. To learn the third technique starts out as before but this time feet don't move. Instead leave your base on the ground and whip your dominant hip in a forwards rotation as you launch the weapon as before. These three techniques will work for any throwing weapon. In the case of throwing stars stand with your dominant leg forward and weapon in your dominant hand. Rock back and bring your hand under your support arm pit across your body, powerfully rock forwards and launch the weapon like a Frisbee. For all throws point your fingers at the target on release for a correct follow through.

The most important thing for learning how to throw weapons is trust in the technique, clear your mind, and don't care. Once the weapon has left your hand there's nothing you can do about it. Hit, miss, stick, or bounce what's important is the weapons still in your hands. Shuriken Jutsu is often referred to as "the art of letting go," because if your holding tension in your body, not confident in your technique, and not using power it'll never work.

The last tip for practicing Shuriken Jutsu is be safe! Eye protection and other safety considerations are very important. I've personally experienced how quickly a shuriken can bounce back and stab the thrower. Throw in a safe direction with a safe backdrop. Make sure everyone around you knows your throwing live blades. And if possible offset the target to a 45 degree angle to you so that if there is bounce back it might go in a safe direction instead of straight back at the thrower.

Training the Brain
July 2012
Monthly Student Newsletter

Martial artists understand the importance of repetition in training and most will tell you that training is as much a mental exercise as a physical workout. This description seems to be intuitive to most. The purpose of this article is to teach you the science of how the human brain and mind work and strategies to get the most out of your training.

Our entire teaching strategy at FTS Inc. revolves around the idea of creating "schema." Schema is the Latin word that "schematic" was derived from. Schematic are basically blue prints of a process or structure. When martial artists are completing repetitions of their movements it's often described as "muscle memory." This description isn't entirely accurate. What repetitions of movement actually does is line up neurons in the brain creating "schema." To understand the difference we must look at the biology of the brain.

The brain has neurons in it. Each neuron is built of a receiver, and transmitter, and a path that a particular message travels down. Each neuron is responsible for conveying 1 part of a motor skill message from the brain to the central nervous system, to the body part(s) involved, and to another neuron so the message can continue.

The problem with learning a new motor skill is that the neurons aren't in order or close to one-another. They are scattered across the brain. As repetitions of a series of motor movements are rehearsed the neurons in the brain line up with each other and get close to each other. The brain will actually change shape. When this happens motor skill responses are fast, powerful, and smooth.

There are two methods for lining up neurons in this way. The first is, as we've discussed above, to complete high number of repetitious movement. Every time the movement is competed the neural pathways for the motor movement in the brain line up and get closer together. This can be painstakingly slow however and takes thousands of repetitions. Most research seems to agree that somewhere between 1000-5000 reps are required to create a new neural pathway for a new motor movement. This is because the brain actually changes shape as the neurons line up.

The second method is to complete the movements while experiencing stress. The brain stem part of the brain, which is attributed to the subconscious mind, doesn't understand the difference between reality and fiction. It assumes everything is real. For this reason a stress exercise can be introduced into training to create the schema with fewer reps. Even though the student knows on a conscious level that they're safe, on a subconscious level they'll believe their life is in danger.

The human brain and mind have adapted so that once a motor response was successful under life or death stress that response goes into storage for the next time. I see a lot of martial artists who don't understand that and only practice in safe, sanitary, environment where there is no stress. The danger with training under stress is that mistakes might get trained into the schema and then be very difficult to train out later.

For this reason the student must begin practicing their movements slow and in control, focusing on every step of the series for technical expertise. Then once a satisfactory level of understanding has been achieved introduce stress to create appropriate responses. Then go back to the beginning and perform the skills with 100% technical expertise. Then introduce the stress again. Using this cycle can greatly increase a students learning and comprehension AND decrease the amount of time to learn a sill.

Using the mind model to explain training schema is convenient for students because it means that they can perform mental repetitions of the techniques even when they're unable to attend a training session. Remember that the part of the brain and mind that perceive stress don't know the difference between reality and fiction. Therefore by mentally rehearsing the series of techniques the schema is built and re-enforced.

Strategies for increasing your ability to learn motor skills should include as many senses as possible. Teaching and learning must contain an audio, visual, and tactile component. As well throughout training stop and ask what the room smells like, tastes like, and what are you feeling. Next keep notes. Keeping notes is an excellent way to access long term memory stores and will reinforce the schema and help line up neurons. Lastly practice in your mind. Close your eyes, imagine the events or situation you're going to respond to, and mentally rehearse the motor skill response. Imaginary training can produce real world results.

Understanding How We Learn
July 2012
Monthly Student Newsletter

I'm constantly surprised at how quickly students can develop knowledge and skill. Regardless of age or natural talent this quarters 32 rank promotions in Martial Arts Division and another 13 certifications in Tactical Division are proof that people are capable of great things when they put their minds to it. The purpose of this article is to teach you how the human brain and mind work and strategies to get the most out of your training.

Our entire teaching strategy at FTS Inc. revolves around the idea of creating "schema." Schema is the Latin word that "schematic" was derived from. Schematic are basically blue prints of a process or structure. From a mind model paradigm we give our students 1 of an infinite number of possibilities in the "when-then" spectrum. Basically we create a blue print for questions. For example, "when someone lunges at me with a knife aimed at my stomach, then I'll move to the side, deflect the knife with my hands, wrap the arm, and leg reap the person to the ground."

The student then begins practicing this series of events slow and in control, focusing on every step of the series for technical expertise. Using the mind model to explain training schema is convenient for students because it means that they can perform mental repetitions of the techniques even when they're unable to attend a training session. By mentally rehearsing the series of techniques the schema is built and re-enforced.

This doesn't explain the need for repetitions or for performance under stress however. To understand why that makes a difference we must look at the biology of the brain. The brain has neurons in it. Each neuron is built of a receiver, and transmitter, and a path that a particular message travels down. Each neuron is responsible for conveying 1 part of a motor skill message from the brain to the central nervous system, to the body part(s) involved, and to another neuron so the message can continue.

The problem with learning a new motor skill is that the neurons aren't in order or close to one-another. They are scattered across the brain. As repetitions of a series of motor movements are rehearsed the neurons in the brain line up with each other and get close to each other. The brain will actually change shape. When this happens motor skill responses are fast, powerful, and smooth.

One of the things that can speed this process up is to perform repetition under stress. The brain stem part of the brain and corresponding sub-conscious mind don't know the difference between a real event and an imaginary event. For this reason stress can be added to the training and the neurons will line up with fewer repetitions and the schema will be created faster.

Strategies for increasing your ability to learn motor skills should include as many senses as possible. Teaching and learning must contain an audio, visual, and tactile component. As well throughout training stop and ask what the room smells like, tastes like, and what are you feeling. Next keep notes. Keeping notes is an excellent way to access long term memory stores and will reinforce the schema and help line up neurons. Lastly practice in your mind. Close your eyes, imagine the events or situation you're going to respond to, and mentally rehearse the motor skill response. Imaginary training can produce real world results.

Take Their Breath Away
October 2012
ILEETA Journal

In a ground fight both combatants will use much more energy to fight. This is due to the fact that each body has more contact with another surface and therefore more drag or friction to overcome while moving and the fact that each movement results in moving not only your own body but also your opponent's. Moving in a ground fight therefore requires more air to be delivered via the lungs to the blood stream to oxygenate the muscles.

Professional fighters and submission fighters have known this for years and have developed strategies to use it to their advantage. Often in a submission grappling match opponent's will attempt to find ways to smother each other. You can imagine in the middle of a ground fight gasping for air and now something is being placed over your nose and mouth.

The same strategy can work for LEO's in ground fights. Often (but not always) it would be inappropriate to strangle an opponent, and some more violent encounters may result in a serious assault but not cross the death/grievous bodily harm threshold. Even in situations where subject's are resisting control but not attempting to assault anyone smothering them can be an appropriate way to distract them from their resistance.

The idea of a smother isn't to render your opponent unconscious. Rather it's to use a smother technique as a distraction. In the case of ground fighting it's highly effective because of increase in oxygen intake discussed above but also because of counter pressure. If you're in a top positions the ground will provide counter pressure. If you're in a bottom position the subject will likely begin moving their head in the direction you're applying the smother technique in order to get away from it.

Simply cupping your hand and pushing it over an opponent's nose and mouth can be really distracting and possibly change their thought process form their illegal activity to simply trying to catch their breath. The same idea can be applied to lying across an adversaries face and pushing your body armour into their nose and mouth. You may find that very quickly they're so busy thinking about breathing that they don't care about hurting or resisting you anymore.

    Remember a few important things though. Like with any use of force application there is a time and a place. Know what the expectations are in your jurisdiction. Also remember that the application of the technique in anything short of a life and death encounter IS NOT to render a subject unconscious or dead but rather to draw their thought process to breathing and not fighting. Once you've accomplished that the window to follow up control techniques is open and the officer should take the opportunity to end the encounter in a lawfully appropriate manner. And lastly whenever applying a smother to someone's nose and mouth there is a chance they're going to try to bite you. Be aware of it and prepared and decide in advance when you're going to take that chance.

Understanding the Center Line
December 2012
FMA Informative

In martial arts training there's a concept referred to as "center line." This concept is usually very well understood by experience martial artists but new students can sometimes struggle to understand what it means. This conceptual article is intended to help new students understand center line and what it's all about and experienced martial artists to be able to pass the information on to newer students.

What is the centerline?

It's the line that runs down the center of the body. Duh! Well not quite that simple. While Center Line does refer a point of reference that runs down the center of someone's body vertically from their head to the ground below them, it can become much more important and difficult than that. When a person is standing perfectly erect this center line can be thought of a line that runs with the spine from looking at the person front or rear. However unlike the spine the center line is straight, not curved, and not able to curve. So when we look at someone from the side we cannot simply pick the spine as a point of reference. Instead the center line when viewed from the side would intersect the spine at various points as the line runs down the perfect center of their body vertically from the top of their head to the ground below them.

It's important to understand that the Center Line runs to the ground below the person because this is how balance manipulation techniques are facilitated. So if I'm standing perfectly up straight the line when run from the center of the top of my skull down through the middle most point in my body and hit the ground between my feet and roughly lined up with my ankles.

The Center Line also refers to most of the vital targets in the body, particularly when it comes to a blade or a bullet. The

Center Line intersects the heart and runs between the lungs. It would intersect intestines and stomach, sit just behind the wind pipe, intersect the brain and run just behind and between the eyes. It would also intersect the reproductive and waste management systems as well as the spine and central nervous system.

Controlling and attacking this line in our opponent's should be one of our major strategies in a fight.

Methods of Attack-Precision Weapons

As briefly mentioned above attacking the Center Line with a precision weapon (I.E. edged weapons and firearms) could be a fast and effective method to stop an attacker. The body is designed to protect this center line starting from the outside working in. In ancient Japan Samurai armour was designed the same way. If you're standing straight up and down arms at your sides, the big muscles and bones in your arms and legs protect this line from attacks on outside angles. The ribs, vertebrae, hips, shoulder blades, and sternum all protect it in the torso from outside angle attacks.

So I guess we're invincible! Not exactly. Generally speaking wherever there is a "hallow" the line can be found very easily with a precision weapon. For example if you put your fingers on your sternum and follow it up to your neck you should feel a small "V" notch in the bone. This hallow indicates that there is no bone to protect the Center Line. A puncture here would be very effective. These hollows can be found all over the body and indicate a weak point in our "armour" as it were. Find any hallow in the body, aim the weapon into the center line, and thrust. Examples include arm pits, clavicle notch, eye sockets, and inner thigh. Thrusting a precision weapon through one of these hallows towards the Center Line will bypass bone and do a lot of soft tissue damage, often in the way of either central nervous system damage or major organ damage.

Part of your blade and firearm training therefore should be targeting these areas and in close quarters understanding how to move the opponent's' limbs and torso to expose them. Blades and bullets don't do well against bone so understand how to get around them to create wounds that are more effective at stopping a threat.

Methods of Attack-Balance Manipulation

Understanding Center Line is crucial in balance manipulation arts such as Judo, Wrestling, and Ju Jutsu. As previously mentioned this line runs right through the body and hits the ground below us between our feet and lined up with our ankles. When we are in balance our head, shoulders, pelvis, knees, and ankles all line up with each other vertically when viewed from the side. The key to balance manipulation (takedowns and throws) is to use shearing force to take two points off center line. Shearing force means and application of energy to any 1 of these 5 points in 1 direction, and an application of energy to any 1 of the remaining in an opposing direction. For instance stand behind a training partner, pull back on their head and push forwards on the back of their knee with your foot and watch what happens. This force should be "pushing" and not "striking" energy however. If you strike one of these points and there's no force to keep it where you moved it to, than that opponent is likely to just correct their posture back to where they were when you started. Pushing energy moves a point of contact to where you want it and keeps it there. Striking energy hits a point of contact and then comes off contact to cycle for the next hit.

A perfect example of this comes from MMA. Watch any UFC event and you'll see countless Double Leg Shots (or Shooting Takedown). In a good Shot the attacker secures his opponent's knees from behind with his hands and pulls them forwards while simultaneously pushes with their shoulders on their opponent's' pelvis. This is an example of Shearing energy through center line on two points of contact and results in a takedown.

Although in these examples I only mention moving forwards and backwards through the opponent's Center Line once you understand the concept there are numerous takedowns that work the same concept laterally through Center Line.

Methods of Attack-Percussion Weapons

A percussion weapon is any weapon that smashes or uses blunt force trauma. Sticks, batons, and body weapons (hands, feet, elbows, knees, head) are all examples. Effecting Center Line with these weapons is much more difficult. A percussion weapon isn't likely to pierce the body and cause internal organ damage because of the body structure discussed above. Percussion weapons are very good however at breaking down that natural suit of armour designed to protect the center line and achieve central nervous system shut down due to blows to the head, pain to psychologically stop an attacker, or breaking down their skeletal system so that they are unable to use limbs to stand or strike and continue their attack.

Attacks, for the most part, change slightly. With a percussion weapon I'm not particularly interested in sneaking behind the bone structure to vital organs. Instead I direct my weapon to or through the Center Line seeking to smash everything and anything in its path. This works very well to capitalize on a person's flinch response. As you swing percussion weapon at someone's Center Line they'll almost always flinch and raise some sort of shield into the path of the weapon to protect themselves. Where an edged weapon might only cause surface wounds through skin and muscle a percussion weapon can break the structure beneath. Sometimes in training I prefer to startle my opponent into a flinch response and then use a combination of strikes on the now exposed limb. It doesn't take long until they change their thought process to one of defense instead of offence.

Using Your Own Center Line

The final, and perhaps most important, point to this discussion is developing discipline to your own Center Line. Often I see beginners throwing wild strikes that are all over the map and leave them exposed to a variety of counters. It is important to understand that while attacking an opponent we should be seeking retention of our own weapons back to our own core.

A great exercise for this is the Balintawak Cuentada Eskrima 12 Basic Strikes drill. The exercise starts off with students establishing their Center Line and every attack goes to, but not through, that Center Line and then returns to the core for weapon retention and cycling purposes.

Often changing the angle of your Center Line relative to your opponent's will open targets and opportunities for attack while moving you out of the way of their attack. In Brazilian Jiu Jitsu before any attack you move your Center Line in relation to your opponent's to open new angles and if you leave your limbs across your own Center Line you usually find yourself submitted shortly thereafter.

Conclusion

The idea of establishing Center Line and understanding how to move it, protect it, and attack it is vital in any martial arts training. Arts such as Wing Chun and Koto Ryu maintain this philosophy for hundreds of years and have it as their very core.

In Filipino martial arts you will find this idea, in some form, in every style and in every skilled artist. Developing discipline to your own core and Center Line should be paramount in your training and understand how to move around, and open up, your opponent's is critical to shut down an attacker in an efficient manner.

The Ethical Warrior
February 2013
Monthly Student Newsletter

Let me begin this article by saying that the idea of the Ethical Warrior is not mine. This is a summarization of the work provided by Shihan Jack Hoban. For more on his work please click here.

Shihan Jacks work and book The Ethical Warrior Values, morals, and ethics for life, work and service has become the base of all classes at FTS Inc. Both in the Tactical Division and the Martial Arts Division.

The Ethical Warrior bases all decisions off 1 Ethic. Notice the use of the word ETHIC, instead of MORAL. An Ethic differs from a Moral in that Morals are things we know to be right and good, Ethics are when we act on it. This is important because it denotes that warriors must Act, not just think and know but not do anything with that knowledge.

The ethic that we base all our decisions on is the Dual Life Ethic. This means that every decision I make I should take into consideration if it will harm my right to life, OR anyone else's right to life. At first glance this seems straight forward but in practice it become much more difficult. For instance how do we create a training program or philosophy that not only protects the students, but also teaches the students to protect everyone else, including people who might be out to hurt them?

It means that before we're allowed to use physical skill on an opponent we must've exhausted all other means of protecting ourselves or those around us. It also means that when we do decide it's time to use physical skill to stop someone we should strive to ensure that it is the least intrusive and damaging option at our disposal. The law says we must pick a reasonable option, but the dual life ethic says we're striving to pick the best option that will result in the least amount of harm.

According to the dual life ethic there must be a loss of innocence before we can use physical methods on an opponent. That is someone's right to life becomes forfeit when they decide to rob an innocent party of their right to life by attempting to hurt them. Again keep in mind however that whatever force we use on an opponent should be the least intrusive possible to protect innocent life.

This model can be used as a general decision making model for day-to-day life decisions. For example a student brought up a temper problem he's having the other day. He said to me that if someone cuts him off in traffic he has a hard time not following the person and fighting them when the get out of their vehicle. Even the best case scenario for my student violates the dual life principle. If he gets in a fight and wins, he has violated someone else's right to life. If he gets in a fight and loses and gets beaten up he placed himself in a decision where his right to life was at risk.

You could apply this decision making process to many decisions. Even J-Walking violates the dual life principle. You are placing yourself and possibly others (i.e. motorists) at risk for serious physical harm and possibly even death.

I highly encourage each reader to check out Shihan Jack's work for yourself. This was a brief summary in my words of the Dual Life Principle and Ethical Warrior. This idea is the base for all of our programs because it gives us a "Moral North" on our compass for life that does not change. The right to life trumps all other rights and provides us guidelines for when we can and when we can't use our skills.

Seeking Martial Artists, not just people who do martial arts
September 2013
Monthly Student Newsletter

People come to the dojo for many reasons. Some seek fitness, some self confidence, and some a hobby. Some people want to test their grit and challenge themselves. Some people show up and just barely put in enough energy to go through the motions, and some take what I'm teaching and make it their life.

This last group of people, the ones who make martial arts a lifestyle, are truly martial artists. The former categories are people who are doing martial arts. There are ways to tell which you are.

If you are constantly making excuses to not train, you're a person who does martial arts. I'm constantly surprised with the excuses I hear. Just the other night a student told me that they couldn't train because they didn't have any clean clothes for after work or any money. And then that same student went out to a bar in clean clothes where I suspect they had to spend at least what a drop in fee costs. This is an excuse to not train.

Excuses to not train really boggle my mind. If we look at other artists, painters, musicians, sculptors, chiefs, etcetera, they strive to find time to practice their art. People who do martial arts seem to constantly strive to find reasons not to.

Recently one of my shodans was on holidays and while on holidays made it part of his trip to visit some martial arts clubs that he was interested in and train. This is a mark of the martial artist. To find reasons to train, not reasons not to train.

Many people can't stay plugged into class for the duration of the class. Not only do their minds wander but they become distracted and training becomes social time. Sometime their whole reason for attending class becomes to see their friends. Turning training time into social time is another indicator that someone is doing martial arts, and isn't a martial artist.

A martial artist values their training time. They might even get upset with people who are distracting the group or "stealing" valuable time by turning class into a social engagement. They want to train. Not only are they able to plug in for the entire class and want to be there with every ounce of their being but they take the lessons with them when they leave.

This brings me to the last indicator of whether you're doing martial arts, or are a martial artist. Many students only train when they're at class. They don't do any homework. Again this really blows my mind that martial arts students think this is acceptable. If you look at other artists (as listed above) they would all practice on their own time. In some cases more than they would practice in class.

A martial artist doesn't even need to be told what or when to practice. They're hunger to understand and get better kicks in and they practice at home at least 1 hour for every hour they're with their instructor, if not more.

As you're reading this you might relate more to the descriptions of someone who does martial arts. That's ok if that's what you want. But if you want to become a martial artist you have to take action. It's not a passive activity. Look for reasons to train, instead of excuses not to, plug into class when you're there, and practicing on your own are three steps to get you there.

The Schools of the Bujinkan
March 2014
Deep Water Magazine

     My personal passion and training experience has been spent in the Bujinkan. Although I cross train in Jeet Kune Do, Brazilian Jiu Jitsu, and systems of Filipino Martial Arts, Bujinkan has been my passion and foundation. The Bujinkan is the largest organization of Ninjutsu training worldwide with just over 250,000 registered students and is comprised of 9 traditional Japanese martial art systems. Ninjutsu is actually a small portion of the training.

     These 9 systems were each their own school, or Ryuha in Japanese, and throughout the course of history were brought together through familial alliances and bonds. Some of the schools were samurai lineage, and some were of ninja origin. Ninjutsu itself didn't emerge as a martial art until after the Tokugawa shogunate in the early 1600's. Before that it existed as stealth training and before that as the philosophy Ninpo, which can actually be found in military records from many different martial arts systems including Ju Jutsu, Karate, Kenjutsu, and other fighting systems of ancient Japan. Takamatsu sensei was the first person to be the soke (grandmaster) in all 9 and he passed the lineages to Hatsumi sensei. Takamatsu sensei used to train the schools independent of each other and would instruct that a particular kata or movement was from a particular school and their names. Hatsumi sensei however blended all 9 into the Bujinkan, sometimes known as Hatsumi Han (Hatsumi house or system). The idea being that a student would learn a certain level of freedom and expression by seamlessly transitioning from 1 style to the next without thinking of it as a "style".
The 9 schools;

     Togakure Ryu Ninpo. 戸隠流 As with most of Ninjutsu the Togakure Ryu is shrouded in mystery. Of the nine schools in Bujinkan this school is the oldest and the foundation.

Up until the year 2000 most training certificates said "Togakure Ryu" on them and not "Bujinkan."

    The Ryuha is thought to have developed in the late 1100's/early 1200's when a samurai retainer, Daisuke Nishina, escaped a battle where his forces were defeated and killed, and fled into the mountains of Iga. There he evaded capture and met a group of monks from China who trained in martial arts on Mount Hiei-zan. He took refuge with them and combined their spiritual training with his own, and their martial art with his own samurai arts. He developed a system of training to defeat samurai and that focused on 18 disciplines.

    The 18 skill sets taught, developed, and refined in the Ryu were; Seishin Teki Kyotyo, or "spiritual refinement", Taijutsu or "unarmed combat", Kenjutsu or "sword art", Bojutsu is the art of "stick or staff fighting" and also includes fighting techniques for fighting with sticks that conceal blades, Shuriken-Jutsu "throwing blades", Yari-Jutsu is the skill of "spear fighting", "Halberd fighting" was known as Naginata-Jutsu, Kusari-Gama "chain and sickle weapons", use of fire and explosives as weapons and distraction devices which was called Kayaku-Jutsu, Henso-Jutsu is the vital ninja skill of "disguise and impersonation", Shinobi-Iri or "stealth and entering methods", Ba-Jutsu, which was all skills and techniques associated with "horsemanship", "water training" or Sui-Ren, the unconventional battle tactics used by ninjas and their understanding of political plots was referred to as Bo-Ryaku, Cho Ho or "espionage", Inton-Jutsu or "escape and concealment", Ten-Mon was used to predict weather patterns that would be most advantageous to a ninja's goals or would threaten their survival, and the final type of training that a ninja received was Chi-Mon or "geography" and was the ability to use the terrain to one's advantage.

    It wasn't until 3 generations after its creation that the system was formalized and the name "Hidden Door School" was created. The name itself eludes to the philosophy of finding the path less travelled and the using the unsuspected strategy to defeat an opponent. As you can see training in the Togakure Ryu could take a lifetime to learn all the different skills!

Gyokko Ryu Koshijutsu. 玉虎流 This school is believed to have been brought to Japan from China by Cho Gyokko during the Tang Dynasty. The name translates to "Jeweled Tiger" school and closely resembles elements of long arm kung fu. The school teaches kosshijutsu, which calls for attacks to the muscles and nerve points of the body, shitojutsu or using the thumbs and fingers for striking and included styles of sword and stick fighting. This Ryu favors circular movement and is one half of a complete fighting system, the other half being linear fighting found in the Koto Ryu.

Koto Ryu Koppojutsu . 虎倒流 This school is the sister style to Gyokko-ryu. This is translated as the "Knocking down the tiger". The school is very linear and favours straight lines as opposed to circular motions. This style of fighting uses kempo (short fist striking) and koppojutsu or "bone law art" which can be broken down into three elements. The first is breaking bones, the second is destroying joints, and the third is manipulating an opponent's skeleton so that they can't maintain balance. This style of fighting is believed to have been brought from Korea to Japan by a monk named Chan Busho. Many movements resemble knife fighting and short blade combat.

Kukishin Ryu Happo Hiken . 九鬼神伝流 Often translated as "Transmission of the Nine Demon Gods School", this school is often described as a battlefield school. Many of the movements take into account body armour and the strategy is often to unbalance your opponent to knock them on their backs. From here a sword or other weapon could've been employed to finish a confrontation. The Kukishin Ryu teaches unarmed fighting (taijutsu), and favours swords (ken jutsu), spears (so jutsu) and short staffs (hanbo jutsu) along with supplemental military strategy and other minor ninjutsu skills.

Kumogakure Ryu Ninpo. 雲隠流 This *ryu* translates to "Hiding in the Clouds" and teaches many taijutsu methods of leaping and uses a specialty spear with a hook that was used as a combat tool and to climb ships. As with all Ninpo schools strategy and mind set are favoured and emphasized over fighting ability. The warriors of this school used armored sleeves to deflect blades and confuse enemies and wore demon masks to frighten and distract them. The sleeves and shin armour usually would've been made out of bo shuriken (throwing spikes) or sanban shuriken (throwing stars) sewn into pockets on the boots or gauntlets. Not only could they deflect weapons but also be accessed as a weapon to launch at opponent's or hit and cut with the weapons in the clothing. It's thought that many of the originators of this school were employed on ships and fishing vessels as protection against pirates and that's why the movements have a gentle swaying motion.

Gikan Ryu Koppojutsu. 義鑑流 **"School of truth, loyalty and justice"** also teaches koppojutsu, the system of unarmed fighting to break bones, joints, or disrupt balance. This school is said to have been developed by a student of the Gyokko-ryu and Koto-ryu and basically combines the strategies and movements of both into his own unique way of moving and fighting. The teachings of the school are very secretive and not taught publically. Many believe the school favoured hidden sword (biken) techniques for its primary weapon. The lineage of this school is in debate and Soke Masaaki Hatsumi's claim that he is the current grandmaster is challenged by Shoto Tanemura. What we do know is that an underlying philosophy in the school was to keep the peace and to never attack first, but rather to use your skill only in defense.

Shinden Fudo Ryu Dakentaijutsu. 神伝不動流 Translates into "immovable heart school" and is the 7th combat school of Bujinkan. This art has two styles of unarmed combat, Jutaijutsu (grappling methods) and Daken Taijutsu (striking methods), although it's believed that originally the school only taught striking methods and it wasn't until much later that the grappling techniques were introduced from another source.

Gyokishin Ryu Ninpo . 玉心流 Translates in "the Jeweled Heart" and mainly concentrates on the espionage skills and other abilities of the ninja than fighting. It is considered a "secret" school and Soke Hatsumi (the current Bujinkan Grandmaster) doesn't disclose its teachings.

Takagi Yoshin Ryu Jutaijutsu. 高木揚心流 Means "High Tree Raised Heart School" and is a system of Ju Jutsu (grappling techniques) which teaches fast breaks, submissions, ground fighting and chokes. In the upper levels of training it is practiced while wearing samurai swords and sometimes employs long staffs as weapons. The school is thought to have been developed for body guards and specializes in applying the grappling techniques with speed so that an opponent cannot counter.

Each of the 9 schools are battlefield arts, meaning that as well as the technical aspects of the school there is an underlying philosophy of tactics and awareness. In many of the kata's from all the schools a turning movement is used (sometimes at the very end) to circumnavigate your surroundings or angles are sought to use opponent's against each other. In each of the 9 weapon skills are taught at the very beginning of the training and continue throughout. This is because many of the body movements take into account the idea that soldiers were trained in weapons first so they were already familiar with moving as though they were armed. Soldiers only fought empty handed in the case of an emergency.

As you can see from the descriptions of the 9 Ryuha of the Bujinkan there is a wide diversity and range of skills. Any one of these 9 schools was, and could still be, taught on its own and a student could spend a lifetime exploring just 1 and mastering its techniques, principles, philosophies, and movements.

Defining Integrity
August 2014
Monthly Student Newsletter

I love being a full time martial arts instructor because it pushes me to challenge barriers every day physically, mentally, and emotionally. One such example happened about 2 weeks ago when one of my senior students and I had a conversation about my integrity. During our discussion he shared that his definition of Integrity is standing beside your word and doing what you said you would do and that sometimes he questions my integrity because he sees me say things and then later change my mind. To him I wasn't standing by my word and therefore my integrity was in question. I asked him what integrity means to him and he equated it to honesty and "doing what you said you were going to do."

This led me on a path of some deep self reflection and exploration. Mainly I was seeking to answer 2 questions. What does Integrity mean and am I a person that has integrity?

Integrity Defined

The first part of my mission was to define integrity. As I started this process I knew I was emotionally invested. I thought the best way to remove my emotion from the equation was to not define integrity as it relates to myself, or even people in general, but to seek a broad understanding of the word.

One definition I found was "the state of being whole and undivided." This is definition relates to structures such as buildings and bridges. This definition to me means that there are many parts to a structure, and each part has to fit together to give the structure its strength, its "structural integrity." This also means that if 1 component of the structure decays, or erodes, or is otherwise compromised then the overall integrity of the structure is compromised. This also means that a structure is built through a process of connecting smaller pieces together over time, and in time needs maintenance on the smaller pieces to stop the entire structure from collapsing.

The Parts

Because I teach Japanese martial arts I started off using the 6 virtues of Bushido for my parts. There are actually 7 but the last one is Gi, which means Integrity. Basically in my mind I thought of building my character like building a structure with 6 floors. When each floor is strong the building, my character, is whole and undivided.

The first and most important part of any physical structure is its foundation. It occurred to me that this is the same for building my character. If a structures foundation is out of alignment even just a minuscule amount then the entire structure will be flawed and fragile.

For my foundation I use the virtue Rei, Respect. I think everything in life boils down to respect. I further break this virtue down to 3 micro virtues, respect for myself, for others, for the environment. I endeavor to respect myself by staying healthy, eating well, exercising regularly, keeping my uniform clean and presentable, and keeping myself groomed and presentable. I show respect for my environment by keeping it clean and pay particular attention to waste management. And I respect others by listening when they speak, not talking about them behind their back, being on time for commitments, and not airing anyone else's business publically. Rei therefore is my foundation to build my character.

Next I employ Makato, Honesty. I think one of the best ways to show respect is to be honest. Again the concept of honesty can have more layers. For example there is being Honest with yourself, your loved ones, employer, and the world in general. I don't think there can be trust without honesty, and if you're not trustworthy you can't be seen to have integrity.

My 3rd floor is Jin, Kindness. I see no reason to cause any unnecessary suffering or pain to any other living thing. What's more is that by being kind to others we are building a stronger community and network around us. Kindness doesn't have to take any resources other than words and the investment can return 1000 fold when you need it most. Kindness also speaks to my own since of confidence. When I don't have anything to hide, when I'm confident in my abilities and in myself, I can let down my walls that protect my own ego. When I am truly confident and happy in my own life it's through Kindness I pick up others around me and help them. By helping others I begin to build a community of likeminded people surrounding me and supporting me.

The opposite of course is cruelty. There is nothing to gain by being cruel. It drives people away and demonstrates to anyone observing you that you don't yet have the personal strength to help others.

The next Bushido Virtue I see in my structure is Yuki, Courage. I think facing our fears and action in the face of fear is one of the most noblest of virtues. I don't think however you can do those things without having self respect and respect for danger (Rei), being honest with yourself and identifying your fears and abilities (Makoto), and letting down your barriers and walls and having a desire to help others (Jin).

I see in many warriors, martial artists and police officers alike, give a certain amount of lip service regarding Yuki, but little action. How often have you been guilty of not having that uncomfortable conversation with someone that you know you should be having? The term Yuki includes the word Energy (Ki). This means to me Kinetic energy, the energy of motion, i.e. of action. Not Potential energy. Therefore in order to have Courage it takes action, not words.

My next level of structure I see in myself is Chugi, Loyalty. I don't really like the word Loyalty however because I've seen it misused and perverted so many times so I use the English word Dedication. The difference for me is that I choose my dedications, but many people may try to trick me into loyalty. For example, "if you loved me (i.e. were loyal to me), than you would do…." But when I dedicate myself to someone, or something, I'm choosing to be all in. It can't be manipulated because it's my choice in the first place.

Dedication isn't just about choosing to be dedicated to people. It can be to an ideal or concept also. I would hope that any law enforcement officer has decided to dedicate themselves to the ideals of Justice, Protection, and Service.

The final Bushido Virtue in the structure is Meiyo, which means Honour. Honour is a hard word to define. One attempt might be Reputation, particularly when someone feels they have to "defend their honour." I either have the reputation of embodying virtue or I do not. It can also be thought of as the previous 5 virtues existing in harmony with each other. I think of my Honour as the penthouse on top of my building. It represents the harmony of the floors below and each floor, from the foundation up, has to be passed through in order to get to the top.

The 7th floor

During this process I decided to add what for me is one more very important virtue, the Japanese word Kenkyo. Kenkyo means Humility, or Modesty. For me personally this is an important virtue because when we're humble we're open to new experiences and fresh ideas. It means we've confronted our demons and we have nothing to hide. We've torn down our walls and barriers and are ready to embrace the human experience. It means we don't have anything to prove and don't waste our time protecting tiny little empires that don't exist or mean anything anyways. For me Kenkyo, Humility, is essential to Integrity.

Conclusion

I think of my character as a structure, and the structure has the parts Respect, Honesty, Kindness, Courage, critical to surround yourself with people who also have integrity and who recognize it and when your structures collapsing will come to your aid and help you rebuild before it completely crumbles.

I believe Integrity is a learned skill. We're not born with it. We learn what it means to be Honest, show Respect, have Courage, be Kind, Dedicate ourselves, have Honour, and be Humble. If Integrity then is a learned skill it should be taught in our schools and at home.

Go with the Flow
September 2014
Deep Water Magazine

     I've been involved in the world of martial arts since I was 16 years old, approximately 19 years now. When I first started in Tae Kwon Do I had an image of what it meant to be a martial artist. I imagined myself always being in control of every situation, being able to defeat any opponent, basically of being the hero in charge of the world.

     A few years ago I attended a swift water rescue training course and I realized that life is more like a river than anything else. There are fast and slow currents, calm and rough waters. There are often hidden perils and dangers, there are times when things occur very swiftly and other times when things are very slow and seem to stand still. Life has a certain flow, just like a river. I believe that once we understand how to read and feel the flow of life, and situations unfolding around us, we can begin to make better decisions that work with that flow, and, just like a boatman navigates a river, we can better navigate those situations and life in general.

     Let me illustrate further by using imagery and analogy to compare life's events to a river and how you can better learn to "go with the flow."

     Rivers flow towards the ocean. A river is described as a body of fresh water flowing towards the ocean. This is an important definition. It denotes that the most important direction of travel for the river is forwards towards a goal or end, as opposed to away from its beginning. When navigating a river it's most important to be looking forwards towards that goal. Not looking behind at where you were. Rivers are often used to reach shorter destinations along their route towards that final destination. Comparing this to the flow of life one could say that life travels towards its final destination, death. And that along the way there are stops and events. Once we accept that we must accept that our attention is forwards towards that final destination, and understand how to use that direction of travel to make those stops along the way.

Rivers display a wide spectrum of intensity. Often the intensity of a river will change while its rate of flow remains the same. For example a river may have a flow rate of 55.15 m3/s. This flow rate remains constant at any point of the river. The intensity of that river can change though at various points along its path. For example if we compare a wide spot in the river, where the width is several meters across, the flow may be described as shallow and slow, meandering even. If we look further downstream of the same river with the same flow rate but reduce the width of the river, then it may described as intense, swift, turbulent, possibly even dangerous or deadly. Even though the flow rate didn't change, the same amount of water is flowing in both cases, the environment in which it flows through had a drastic effect on how it's interpreted. We can compare this analogy to our own lives. We age at a constant rate. Time doesn't speed up or slow down. The flow rate of our lives stays the same. What changes however are the environments that we flow through. Depending on those environments we can interpret life as slow, shallow, boring, or we can experience danger, swift unfolding events, possibly with deadly consequences.

You don't know what's around the next bend. When navigating a river a boatman can never be certain of what's around the next bend. Blind spots inhibit our abilities to see what the future is going to hold. Even an experienced boatman who's navigated the same river many times can never be 100% sure of the next bend. Has the bank changed, are there debris, are there other boats in the way, what changes are there in the environment ahead? We just explored how those changes in environment change how we interpret the intensity of the river. Again this is just like our own lives and especially the events that unfold in law enforcement. Just like the boatman as we navigate a situation we can't know what the next bend will bring. All we know is where we are right now, in this instant. Just like on the path of a river, the environment and dangers of that environment can change in a split second with little or no warning.

Rivers have a lifecycle. The lifecycle of a river can be compared to one of a human, especially experienced in martial arts. Young rivers are usually described as having high narrow banks with swift moving water. Mature rivers are generally wider and slower, and old rivers can be described as flood planes, very wide and slow moving. Just like the training progression of a martial artist. People new to training technique to technique, or sometimes even style or schools get switched every couple months, and often hurry into things and making mistakes that could prove fatal. Mature students have learned to slow down, see more of the big picture, and not rush into conflict, and very experienced students have a wide point of view, seeing the big picture and taking in the environment, taking time to make decisions.

Rivers have rapids. Rapids in water are where the river experiences an increase in velocity and turbulence. They are caused by 3 things, obstructions under the surface of the water, change in river bed height, and confluence, when multiple bodies of water meet each other and run together. Just like in life obstructions lying under the surface, sudden changes, and multiple lives coming together, can all cause turbulence.

If, like me, you subscribe to the belief that life can be like a river, then we can apply similar imagery and analogy to look at strategies for "going with the flow."

Look ahead, not behind. Remember that the river, like life, flows forwards towards its goal. Therefore we are better served focusing our attention ahead of where we are, instead of behind us at where we've been. We must remain mindful of our goals. It's ok to set waypoints along the way, to turn a long journey into the accumulation of several smaller ones, and to strategically place those stops for maximum benefit.
Our life moves forwards at a constant rate. Understanding that what's happening in our life, the environments we're in, and the

events unfolding around us, will cause us to interpret this rate differently. When the environments calm and we're meandering we should capitalize that opportunity for growth, reflection, research, and rest. When we're rushing through a dangerous, rapidly changing, swift, turbulent environment we must stay focused on the task at hand. Successfully navigating that environment will return us to a calm operating environment.

We must be prepared for the unknown. Because we have no idea what the futures going to hold, or even what the next few moments could reveal, we must remain prepared to deal with an unknown. Conflict and combat are very chaotic at times. Thinking you know what's going to happen next is a dangerous lie to tell yourself. Instead be prepared to have to deal with an unknown danger or circumstance. Prepare your body and mind through training and mental rehearsal to observe rapidly changing events, orientate yourself to those events, select a desirable course of action, execute that plan by way of motor movement, evaluate the outcome, and repeat as necessary. If we assume that we know what's happening we may ignore observations that indicate anything other then our assumption. This may be very dangerous and even fatal. If we accept however that we don't know what's behind the next bend in the river, then we're constantly engaged in active observation and prepared to deal with unknowns.

Prepare for rapids. Be prepared for when obstructions under the surface, when there are sudden changes in the environment, or when multiple lives come crashing together with velocity, energy, and turbulence, by learning what the warning signs of these events are. Apply science and training just like a boatman does in his craft. Learn the most desirable skills and methods for dealing with those rapids. Practice and hone those skills to perfection.

Accept that you cannot control the river. The biggest part of learning to "go with the flow" is accepting and admitting that you cannot control all of the people, all of the situations, and all of the environments around you. It's true that there are techniques and actions that have a certain typical response, but nothing is ever 100%. Assuming that we can control these things is foolhardy and dangerous. Instead accept that the only thing you can control is yourself. Once we accept that then we also accept responsibility for our own emotions, responses to those emotions, our training, our careers, our lives. Then we can apply ourselves in this turbulent river of life. Swift water rescue expert Derek Holmes once said, "You don't conquer a river. She just let's you play in her for awhile."

Learn to swim!!! From time to time while navigating the river of life things may become so turbulent and violent that we find ourselves thrown from our boats! If you've only invested time learning how to boat what are you going to do in that emergency situation? Quit likely drown. If, however, we accept that life might throw certain situations at us, and we train for those worst case scenarios, then we have a better chance of making it downstream to safety. If we're so arrogant as to assume that nothing can happen to us, that we're in total control, that we'll never be tossed into the water, then when it does happen we're facing deadly consequences.

Enjoy the ride. One of the best parts about swift water boat work is the ride. As the flow of the river takes you closer to your destination you truly get to experience and marvel some beautiful, often breath taking, moments. If we're so caught up worrying about the turbulent times ahead, or the ones we just passed through, then we can lose sight of the good times we're experiencing right now. Likewise if we're in turbulent times right now, understanding that we have to apply ourselves physically and mentally to get through them to enjoy the meandering beauty on the other side, can give us the motivation to keep going.

For me comparing life to a river and applying the principles or swift water boating and rescue to my life has truly helped me to understand better how to remain satisfied in my life. It's helped me to not stress about things I have no control over. It's helped me to learn to enjoy my downtime and the things that are truly important. It's helped me to understand better how to train and prepare for the dangers of my occupation. It's helped me to stay relaxed, but prepared and alert. If there's one thing I could pass onto the future generations of martial artists it would be, "Learn to go with the flow."

www.ingramcontent.com/pod-product-compliance
Lightning Source LLC
Chambersburg PA
CBHW022053160426
43198CB00008B/216